Fifty Years Faithful

Fifty Years Faithful

THE STORY OF PRESBYTERIAN HOMES

David W. Johnson

Edited by
Michele Hodgson

AFTON HISTORICAL SOCIETY PRESS

Photographs and illustrations for FIFTY YEARS FAITHFUL were provided by Presbyterian Homes & Services, with additional photographs from the following sources:

Andersen Corporation, Bayport, Minnesota

Katherine B. Andersen (page 75).

James J. Hill Reference Library, St. Paul, Minnesota

James J. Hill, 1916 (page 89).

Minnesota Historical Society, St. Paul, Minnesota

The House of Hope Presbyterian Church, St. Paul, Minnesota (page 13);
Gideon H. Pond and Samuel W. Pond (page 48);
Bloomington, postcard ca. 1985, photograph collection (page 48).

Private collection

Hill family farm (1886) by J. Chelminski (page 89).

Scott Streble Photographer, Minneapolis, Minnesota

Boutwells Landing (front cover);
The Farmstead at Andover (page 64);
Boutwells Landing fountain (page 75);
SummerWood of Chanhassen (page 83);
Presbyterian Homes of Bloomington (page 85);
The Farmstead at Andover (back cover).

Gen Wilhelmson, Stillwater, Minnesota

Dorothy and Ed Reid (page 25).

FRONT COVER: *Boutwells Landing in Oak Park Heights, Minnesota.*
HALF-TITLE: *Stained-glass window, Presbyterian Homes of Roseville, Minnesota.*
FRONTISPIECE: *Groundbreaking for the Presbyterian Home in Arden Hills, Minnesota.*
BACK COVER: *The historic round barn at The Farmstead at Andover, Minnesota; stained-glass chapel windows at Boutwells Landing, Oak Park Heights, Minnesota.*

First edition

Edited by Michele Hodgson
Designed by Mary Susan Oleson
Production assistance by Beth Williams
Printed by Pettit Network Inc., Afton, Minnesota

Library of Congress Cataloging-in-Publication Data

Johnson, David W., 1940-
Fifty years faithful : the story of Presbyterian Homes / by David W. Johnson; edited by Michele Hodgson.— 1st ed.
p. cm.
ISBN-13: 978-1-890434-70-0 (hardcover : alk. paper)
ISBN-10: 1-890434-70-1 (hardcover : alk. paper)
1. Presbyterian Homes and Services—History. 2. Retirement communities. 3. Life care communities. 4. Nonprofit organizations. I. Title: 50 years faithful. II. Hodgson, Michele. III. Title.

HV1454.J645 2005
362.61'06'073—dc22

2005016173

Printed in China

AFTON HISTORICAL SOCIETY PRESS
P.O. Box 100, Afton, MN 55001
800-436-8443
aftonpress@aftonpress.com
www.aftonpress.com

Presbyterian Homes & Services

MISSION STATEMENT

Our mission is to provide a broad continuum of care to older adults. The services provided will be of the highest quality and designed to promote independence, dignity, and well-being. The emphasis will be on innovation and leadership in providing compassionate and highly competent care with the inspiration of God's love and word.

The logo of Presbyterian Homes is based on the philosophy of "home" under God's loving care. "Home" is where there is love, care and comfort, kindness, understanding, and respect. A Christian home adds the great depth of God's love and character. Words that are said, jobs that are done, attitudes that are expressed should reflect God's love. Presbyterian Homes is a "home" with these special dimensions. The shape of the logo, including the cross, was taken from the roofline of the Putnam Memorial Chapel at the Arden Hills campus. The three houses represent the three facets of service provided by Presbyterian Homes: retirement living, nursing care, and community services.

Presbyterian Homes board of directors, 1960. Back row from left: John Winn, Earl H. Eide, Reverend Harry Dodgson, Dr. Irving Adams West, H. Trevor Drake, Reverend Gilbert J. Kuyper, John A. Thompson. Seated from left: Mrs. Harold W. Lee, Mrs. C. E. Scott, Mrs. E. G. Booth, Mrs. Alfred Broback, Mrs. A. B. T. Moore.

CONTENTS

A Heart for Excellence

PHS president Dan Lindh.

SINCE ITS FOUNDING in 1955, Presbyterian Homes & Services has been blessed with both the opportunity and the resources to serve older adults. Through generous private donations and public funding, we continue to broaden the reach of our services in Minnesota, Wisconsin, Iowa, and beyond. Through skilled and compassionate employees, we continue to deliver high-tech services with a personal approach to meeting the ever-changing needs of our residents. The dedicated commitment of our employees—their "heart for excellence"—is evident as they attend to the physical, emotional, social, and spiritual needs of all who are a part of the Presbyterian Homes family.

Though Presbyterian Homes & Services has grown and changed considerably over the past half century, we remain faithful to our original call: to help older adults through the inspiration of God's love. The ways in which we serve will continue to evolve as we keep pace with changes in health care, technology, and housing needs, but our directive remains the same. The focus of our ministry-based work is unwavering, and it guides our every effort in making a difference in the lives of those we serve. We are blessed to be a blessing to others.

In *Fifty Years Faithful,* we honor our organization's founders—Irving Adams West, Edwin Kagin, Lillias Joy, and their many fine associates—who answered the call to service and gave it a firm foundation. We honor our donors, who support our growing endeavors to build on that foundation. We honor our partners, who collaborate with us on state-of-the-art continuum of care centers. We honor our employees and volunteers, who combine the technology of the future with the traditions of our past. And we honor our residents and their families, who remind us in ways great and small that our work has purpose and meaning.

We thank the many individuals who made *Fifty Years Faithful* a reality: Jean Greener, our director of church and community relations, who kept watch over the multifaceted project to ensure its quality; author David W. Johnson, who immersed himself in our archives to record fifty years of accomplishments; writer Biloine Young, who interviewed key individuals whose anecdotes tell the personal side of those accomplishments; and Afton Historical Society Press, particularly publisher Patricia Johnston and designer Mary Susan Oleson, who, with editor Michele Hodgson, took the best of our ideas, images, and words to create a book that we hope will inspire future generations to continue this important mission. We are also grateful to the many others, unnamed here, who generously contributed to making this book possible.

As we commemorate the fiftieth anniversary of Presbyterian Homes & Services, we give thanks above all to God—for guiding our hands to skillfully serve, for lifting our hearts to compassionately attend, and for strengthening our resolve to consistently answer the call.

Dan Lindh
PRESIDENT AND CEO
PRESBYTERIAN HOMES & SERVICES

The first Presbyterian Home opened on June 15, 1955, in Arden Hills, Minnesota.

A Time for Every Purpose

To every thing there is a season, and a time for every purpose under heaven.

Ecclesiastes 3:1

THE PURPOSE OF Presbyterian Homes—to meet the needs of retiring pastors and missionaries after a lifetime of service—was inspired by a call to serve others out of gratitude for God's goodness. That purpose was embodied in 1955 in the organization's first community in Arden Hills, Minnesota.

For fifty years, that sense of purpose has guided the growth of Presbyterian Homes. What began as a single campus in one state for thirty of God's servants has evolved into more than thirty communities for 8,000 older adults of all backgrounds, not just in Minnesota but in Wisconsin and Iowa and beyond. Though the amenities of the campuses have changed, the compassion behind the care remains the same. The PHS mission statement of today reflects the values of the organization from its inception: "The services provided will be of the highest quality and designed to promote independence, dignity, and well-being. The emphasis will be on innovation and leadership in providing compassionate and highly competent care with the inspiration of God's love and word."

Among those inspired individuals who founded Presbyterian Homes was Dr. Irving Adams West. From the time he was a fledgling minister on horseback until he retired as pastor of one of America's most influential Presbyterian congregations, Dr. West believed in the power of human possibility through God's love. On the wall of his office at the House of Hope Presbyterian Church in St. Paul hung a written reminder of his personal philosophy, taken from St. Augustine: "Do what you can and then pray that God will give you the power to do what you cannot." He followed these words of wisdom throughout a long and fulfilling career.

Born in 1904 in Craig, Missouri, Irving Adams West grew up the son and great-grandson of Presbyterian ministers. He spent his boyhood in rural Iowa, where his father, Dr. R. Bruce West, was pastor to seven successive congregations. After Irving West graduated from Coe College in Cedar Rapids, Iowa, the tall young man with striking good looks entered Princeton Theological Seminary. While at Princeton, he helped establish a mission church, the Grand Street Chapel, in Rahway, New Jersey, near Newark; he was also in charge of youth work at Rahway's Second Presbyterian Church. While still a seminarian, he began his ministry in Canada in 1927, riding from one church to another on horseback.

After his ordination by the Cedar Rapids Presbytery in 1929, Dr. West became pastor of First Presbyterian Church in Harrisburg, Illinois, and moderator of the Cairo Presbytery. During a vacation in 1932 in Yellowstone National Park, the twenty-eight-year-old pastor (and avid fisherman and outdoorsman) met his future wife, Virginia. At Harrisburg, Dr. West greatly increased membership, adding as many new members as there were existing members when he arrived. He did the same (while reducing debt) at Albany Park Presbyterian Church in Chicago, where he ministered from 1936 to 1940. At the same time, he was elected to the Executive Council of the Presbytery of Chicago. His gift for financial management and leadership was again realized during his three years at Central Presbyterian Church of Zanesville, Ohio, where he also became active in the Muskingum County Ministerial Association and in the Chaplain Reserve Corps.

Dr. West answered the call in 1943 to minister at the House of Hope Presbyterian Church in St. Paul, Minnesota. Over the next twenty-six years—the longest tenure of any pastor at the venerable church—he brought his considerable marketing, leadership, and fund-raising talents to bear on his pastoral work. Early on, he broadcast a weekly radio spot and published a brochure on the church's history. He preached straightforward solutions for common but complex problems. Over the years, membership at the church doubled. He served as director of the National Presbyterian Church Foundation and served on Presbyterian and National Council of Churches committees.

The House of Hope Presbyterian Church, St. Paul, Minnesota.

When it came to fundraising, Dr. West was, in a word, gifted. Within five years of his arrival at the House of Hope Presbyterian Church, donations for expenses more than doubled and benevolence gifts tripled. By the time he retired in 1969, he had completed a $1 million expansion program. His style was aggressive and direct. "When you saw Dr. West coming," said a close friend and former parishioner, "you knew you might as well get out your checkbook." It was a talent that Dr. West used to great advantage when furthering the mission of Presbyterian Homes.

Many years into his ministry, Dr. West told a colleague that he had entered the profession under the inspiration of the Buchmanite and Oxford movements. "The purpose of these movements was complete surrender to the will of God and the guidance of the Spirit," he explained, "and I start each day seeking to do what I think the Holy Spirit wants me to do." He saw the same force at work in the evolution of Presbyterian Homes. "We have tried to be obedient to the heavenly vision," he observed. "This is the reason the Home has gone forward."

Daniel A. Lindh has become the standard bearer in that forward march. Back in 1976, Lindh was a fresh-faced graduate of Bethel College in St. Paul when he was offered an accounting job at Presbyterian Homes. He had another, better-paying prospect, so in true number-crunching fashion, he drew up a list of pros and cons. Conscience, a sense of faith, and a desire to serve won out. Thirty years later—after rising from accountant (adding duties as Sutton Place resident caretaker) to chief financial officer to CEO of Presbyterian Homes & Services—Lindh is steadfastly guided by those same principles.

Like Dr. West, Lindh is the son of a minister. Lindh's father, an educated Swedish immigrant, and his mother, a nurse, both modeled a strong work ethic every day. Like Dr. West, Lindh has deftly guided the growth and financial future of Presbyterian Homes. Like Dr. West, Lindh is faithfully committed to the organization's purpose.

"People sometimes ask, What does it take to achieve high quality on a consistent basis?" he says. "The real key is to focus on *purpose*. . . . When you focus on function, the best you get is 100 percent compliance. High quality comes from function, but it also comes from the heart. We try to engage each employee every day with our *purpose*. . . . We do it by encouraging employees to exercise their gifts in a way that reaches out from the heart, to do whatever they think is appropriate and meaningful to help meet the needs of residents. . . . The *how* should vary; the *purpose* stays the same."

Presbyterian Homes senior management staff, front row from left: Mark Meyer, Duane Larson, Phil Hanson. Middle row from left: Val Alt, Cathy Bergland, Martha Hurr, Beckie Conway, Angie Swetland. Back row from left: Paul Gilje, Walt Zimmermann, Dan Lindh, Lee Osterberg.

Since its founding half a century ago, Presbyterian Homes & Services has stayed true to its purpose: to serve older adults "with the inspiration of God's love and word." The themes of Ecclesiastes inspired this telling of the PHS story. The organization's time to sow arrived when the seed for a simple retirement community was planted. Its time to heal began with the commitment to provide health care as well as housing. Its time to embrace diverse needs of older adults led to a building up of services. And its time to reap that which was planted has been enriched by other providers who share the PHS mission.

This is the story of that mission—of compassionate and competent service to older adults, of innovation and leadership, of inspiration to do God's work. This is the story of remaining fifty years faithful to that mission. This is the story of Presbyterian Homes & Services.

Members of the Knox Presbyterian Church in St. Paul arrive at the Presbyterian Home in Arden Hills, Minnesota, to give residents a ride to services.

Fifty Years Faithful

CHAPTER ONE

A Time to Sow

PLANTING THE SEED

EARLY IN HIS PASTORATE at the House of Hope Presbyterian Church, Dr. Irving Adams West began promoting the idea of a home for the aged in Minnesota. He became interested in the care of the elderly because of his parents, who had always lived in houses provided by the churches his father served. Never having owned their own home, his parents would need a place to live after completing their ministry in Iowa. West envisioned them moving to Minnesota to live in a retirement home developed by the Presbyterian church. In 1946, acting at Dr. West's urging, the Synod of Minnesota of the United Presbyterian Church appointed a committee to study the matter of establishing a home for elderly Presbyterians in the state. Support from the Synod was important as Presbyterian Homes was being formed. The seed had been planted.

Chairing the committee was the multi-credentialed Dr. Edwin Kagin. Born in Germany and raised in Kentucky, Reverend Kagin spent fourteen years as a missionary in Korea. After earning graduate degrees from Princeton and Boston Universities, he became chair of the religion department at Macalester College in St. Paul. His expertise on the work of Minnesota's early Presbyterians and his service to the St. Paul Council of Christian Education, the St. Paul Presbytery, and the Synod of Minnesota made Dr. Kagin an excellent choice to head the Presybterian Homes committee.

In 1947, he and committee members Dr. C. A. Arnold, C. E. Woodward, and R. M. Brockman recommended that a Presbyterian home for the aged be established, in particular for retiring ministers and missionaries. In 1948, Dr. Kagin became chair and president of the Presbyterian Homes board. Discussions about an appropriate site for the home progressed slowly over the next four years, however, until Dr. Kagin urged Dr. West to become the board's president. On September 1, 1952, Presbyterian Homes of the Synod of Minnesota was incorporated. Dr. West envisioned building a retirement home on a lot behind the House of Hope Presbyterian Church, but that would have required purchasing and demolishing several nearby homes. The trustees turned their attention to finding lakeshore property that might include a house that could be appropriately renovated. But such properties proved either too expensive or poorly located. Amid their growing discouragement, church elder Lillias Joy offered to donate about twenty acres of land in memory of her brother Charles, also a church elder. The land overlooked Lake Johanna in Arden Hills, a suburb north of St. Paul.

DONOR PROFILE
Lillias Joy

Although she's best remembered for helping Presbyterian Homes establish its first home for older adults, Lillias Joy dedicated her life to teaching children. After graduating from the University of Minnesota, she taught mathematics at the Loomis School for girls, which became part of the Summit Schools in St. Paul. For much of her life, she also taught Sunday school at the House of Hope Presbyterian Church. After she and three other church members were inspired to memorize the Sermon on the Mount, Miss Joy provided the funds to present Bibles to any other members of the congregation who did the same.

Born in 1882 in Wells River, Vermont, Lillias Joy was six when her family moved to Minnesota. She loved to sail, play tennis, and ride horseback, and although she always had a car at her disposal through her father's Packard dealership, "she never rides anywhere if she can walk," observed a friend. She traveled extensively, mostly to missions and once in the company of the famed Mayo brothers through the Panama Canal. For fifty years, she invited toddlers from the church to her home for an annual ice-cream social. Late in life she returned to teaching as a tutor. Lillias Joy died in 1978, at the age of ninety-five. She never got around to moving to Presbyterian Homes, saying, "I'll do that when I get old."

Benefactor Lillias Joy.

PRESBYTERIAN HOMES OF ARDEN HILLS (PRESBYTERIAN HOME, LAKEVIEW, JOHANNA SHORES), 1955

Groundbreaking for the Presbyterian Home, a thirty-unit community with a communal dining room, took place on June 17, 1954. The cornerstone for the $300,000 structure was laid on November 21, 1954, and the building opened on June 15, 1955. Arthur L. Breidenbach was the home's first superintendent; Margaret Paden was its first resident.

As the widow of a Presbyterian minister, Margaret Paden was a typical early resident of the home. She grew up a member of the Amboy Presbyterian Church in southern Minnesota, where she taught Sunday school and met T. Ross Paden. After his graduation from Princeton Theological Seminary, they began their life together in service to Presbyterian churches in Pennsylvania. In 1908 Reverend Paden accepted a call to First

Presbyterian Church of Mankato, Minnesota; seventeen years later, the couple moved to the Bryn Mawr Presbyterian Church in Minneapolis. In 1930 Reverend Paden became pastor of the Lexington Parkway Presbyterian Church in St. Paul, where his pastorate was cut short by his death in 1933.

Early resident Margaret Paden.

Even before the Presbyterian Home was ready for occupancy, Margaret Paden made a visit to choose her room. She quickly decided on one overlooking Lake Johanna and with easy access to a porch at either end of the corridor. At nine o'clock in the morning on the appointed day, she appeared with her baggage, a favorite easy chair, her writing desk, and a cherished lamp. Her neighbors—mostly women—were retired missionaries, schoolteachers, and pastors or their widows.

In June 1957, Superintendent Breidenbach described "Life in the Home" in his Presbyterian Homes newsletter column: "We have twenty-eight women and ten men who are now residing at the Home. . . . The living rooms are used for musicals, choral groups, study club, church services, games, and jig saw puzzles. . . . We have a television set in each living room. . . . Three excellent meals are served daily. Incidentally, every one of our residents has gained weight since coming to the Home." Sunday afternoon chapel services, accompanied by local church choirs, were led by ministers of the Presbytery.

By April 1960, the newsletter carried admission criteria for prospective residents: $750 for a one-time admission fee, $125 for monthly room and board. For their first six months, residents were on probation, during which they "must be able to make a satisfactory social adjustment to the other residents of the Home." In December 1961, the newsletter reported on the home's social activities, including croquet, rides into the country, afternoon tea, musicals, book reviews, travel lectures (with the occasional slide show by Dr. West), and "moving pictures." In May 1962, a report on the Home's crafts program indicated that a "Mr. Larson, the only man in our class, has made very attractive tiled trivets and jewelry boxes for his daughters-in-law. . . . I'll bet he never expected to be making jewelry boxes out of fishing tackle boxes in Minnesota."

EARLY EXPANSION

Over the next two decades, Presbyterian Homes took root and grew vigorously. The Presbyterian Home (renamed Lakeview around 1978, Johanna Shores in 1984, then Presbyterian Homes of Arden Hills in 1992) expanded almost continuously through four construction projects. In 1958, the first housing addition—consisting of ten rental apartments and a four-bed infirmary—was opened. Built for approximately $100,000, the addition was given by Molly Clements in memory of her husband, Melville Clements, an elder at the House of Hope Presbyterian Church. A second housing addition, the Irving Adams West Wing, opened in 1963. The $800,000 project accommodated forty residents and twenty infirmary beds.

The third project was a long-awaited free-standing chapel, built in 1966 with a $50,000 lead gift from Molly Clements Putnam in memory of her second husband, Douglas Putnam. Putnam was a cofounder of Waldorf Paper Company in St. Paul who, for twenty-five years, served as the clerk of session at the House of Hope Presbyterian Church. Fellow parishioner Robert Ackermann designed the 125-seat interfaith chapel, which is as ecumenical in its architecture as it is in its services. Its sanctuary blends elements of Italian, German, and French Gothic design, while its façade is reminiscent of English, Norman, and Tudor styles. The steeply pitched cedar-shake roof evokes a thirteenth-century Scandinavian influence.

The Irving Adams West Wing was added to the Arden Hills campus in 1963.

Until a freestanding chapel could be built, services were held in the Home.

EMPLOYEE PROFILE
Chaplain Bruce Ervin

Dr. Irving Adams West was known to deliver meditations in Arden Hills' Putnam Memorial Chapel every weekday for more than fifteen years. Nowadays, several ministers conduct a variety of interfaith services at the chapel—including memorial services and the occasional wedding—under the leadership of Reverend Bruce Ervin, director of spiritual care at Presbyterian Homes of Arden Hills. Residents physically unable to attend the services can tune in via closed-circuit television; memory care residents may also participate in services tailored just for them.

Reverend Ervin, who began his ministry at Arden Hills in 2000, sees a spiritual beauty in the residents he serves. "I appreciate the depth of their life experiences and their faithfulness to the Lord," he says. He also appreciates the beauty of the Putnam Memorial Chapel, which he describes as "a beautiful and perfect space. . . . [It] has the character of a sanctuary."

The Putnam Memorial Chapel opened in 1966 on the Arden Hills campus.

Newton Wing was the fourth major addition to the Arden Hills campus during its first twenty years of existence. In 1971, ninety-six-year-old Millicent Newton turned the first clump of earth for the 117-unit wing from her wheelchair using a long-handled chrome spade that was specially designed for the groundbreaking. A bequest of $500,000 from her sister Carrie Newton served as the lead gift for the $2.3 million Newton Wing, which contained thirty-one skilled care beds and twenty-nine intermediate skilled care beds in addition to fifty-seven residential apartments.

Other improvements to the Home included landscaping in 1962, with donations from the estate of Grace Bee Whitridge, a long-time faculty member of Macalester College and member of the House of Hope Presbyterian Church congregation. The grounds were further beautified in 1964 when the Newton sisters donated parkland on Lake Johanna in memory of their parents, Lester and Letta Newton. Newton Park transformed a swamp dotted with decaying shacks and Quonset huts into a place of great natural beauty. The Newton sisters also supplied the campus with its air-conditioning system.

DONOR PROFILE
The Newton Sisters

The Newton sisters—Bessie, Carrie, and Millicent—were lifelong members of the House of Hope Presbyterian Church in St. Paul. Bessie was survived by Carrie and Millicent, whose legacy of generosity helped shape the early history of Presbyterian Homes.

Their story is something of a fairytale. Former schoolteachers Carrie and Millicent Newton retired to the Presbyterian Home, having led a frugal existence to guard against the day when illness might render them destitute. "And then a nurse in the home found some papers," said Reverend K. William Hagstrom, then the superintendent of Presbyterian Homes. "She told the sisters they were possessors of gilt-edged investments made by their parents, and as a result, the ladies who had feared they would be paupers discovered they were virtually millionaires."

Carrie Newton died in 1964, just days before Newton Park on the Arden Hills campus was dedicated. Millicent Newton died ten years later, in 1974, at the age of 100.

EARLY VOLUNTEERISM

Dr. West recognized that the future of Presbyterian Homes depended on the contributions of dedicated volunteers. With characteristic speed, he began to put a volunteer structure in place that would nourish the growing organization. In 1957, Dr. West's wife, Virginia, assisted by Vernus Hildebrand and Marge Douglas, began a Mission Sewing Group with the residents. By the early 1960s, volunteers arranged and staffed Dr. West's

Putnam Memorial Chapel.

Chaplains group, front row from left: Janet Shannon, Floyd Hackett, Nancy Anderson, Donald Krause, Bruce Nelson. Back row: Rick Miller, Bill Chadwick, Gene Sipprell, Bruce Ervin, Howard Herringshaw. Not pictured: Ellen Capecchi, Carol Collins.

Millicent Newton reviews blueprints with nurse Esther Brown and Dr. Irving Adams West.

semiannual open houses, which served both as social gatherings and marketing events.

In 1970, Dr. West announced the formation of a Volunteer Steering Committee. At its helm were Dorothy Reid and Claudia Breidenbach, wife of Presbyterian Home superintendent Arthur Breidenbach. Dr. West's announcement of Reid's appointment came as a surprise to her. "I said, '*What* did you say, Dr. West?'" she recalls. "Oh," he replied, "didn't Ed tell you?" Dorothy was an obvious choice for the position; she and her husband, Ed, had been close to donor Lillias Joy and to Dr. West, who had married them and baptized their four children. Dorothy immediately went to work, persuading women's groups at neighboring churches—Episcopalian and Lutheran as well as Presbyterian—to join her efforts. Inspired by its slogan, "Volunteers Make the Difference," the committee began overseeing clerical tasks and mending drives. They stocked a "Country Store" at the Home with snacks, sundries, books, and magazines. Mostly, says Dorothy, volunteers did (and still do) whatever residents needed, whether feeding them a meal, reading them a book, or just being "a companionable presence."

VOLUNTEER PROFILE
Dorothy and Ed Reid

The passage of time hasn't diminished Dorothy and Ed Reid's commitment to Presbyterian Homes & Services. These longtime volunteers are still at it decades after they first became involved: Dorothy waits on customers at the Market at Boutwells Landing in Oak Park Heights, Minnesota, while Ed serves on the Presbyterian Homes Foundation board.

Helping others move into Presbyterian Homes convinced the Reids to do the same. "We had cleared out enough houses that we decided not to leave that problem to our children," Dorothy says. She and Ed helped their mothers move into Arden Hills, as well as their friends (and PHS donors) Dolores and John Holl. The Reids moved into Boutwells Landing in 2001. Ed, a landscape architect and former owner of Park Nursery, designed much of the landscaping on several Presbyterian Homes campuses.

The Reids laud the PHS philosophy of caring for its residents. "If something happens to one of us, all the help is right here. We don't have to call our kids," Dorothy says. "It is like a family."

VOLUNTEER PROFILE
George and Cheryl Knieriemen

When George and Cheryl Knieriemen moved from New Jersey to Minnesota in 1968, the Presbyterian Home in Arden Hills gained two of its staunchest allies. As pastor of North Como Presbyterian Church, Reverend Knieriemen got professionally acquainted with the Home through church members who were residents and through the services he conducted there. He also got to know the home personally when his parents moved there in 1971. Cheryl Knieriemen's involvement began in 1978, when she and Katherine "Tinker" Roe shared the title of volunteer coordinator.

The Knieriemens have long since retired, but they volunteer regularly at Arden Hills. Cheryl reads to residents and offers companionship; George presents the news to the Home's current events group. "I have always been impressed with the high quality and caring spirit that surrounds the Home," Cheryl says. The Knieriemens are glad to be a part of that mission.

CHANGING OF THE GUARD

In 1965, the Reverend Harry Dodgson became superintendent of Presbyterian Homes upon the retirement of Arthur Breidenbach. "That you may be free from worldly care and avocation," Reverend Dodgson's contract read, "you are to receive an annual salary of nine thousand three hundred dollars. . . . In addition, you are to receive free use of the superintendent's home, all utilities, [a pension plan], and one month's vacation annually." Reverend Dodgson served until May 1970, when the Reverend K. William Hagstrom succeeded him.

In its early years, the Presbyterian Homes board was involved in the most miniscule aspects of administration. Members reviewed all admission applications, maintained a waiting list of prospective residents, recruited

Volunteers Dorothy and Ed Reid.

Volunteers George and Cheryl Knieriemen.

Music played a large role in the social activities of the Home.

The Home's first communal dining room.

and hired employees, and made major and minor architectural, construction, and landscaping decisions. A snapshot of life at the Home, recorded by Reverend Dodgson in the board minutes of March 24, 1969, provides a typical view of the intimate atmosphere that flourished at that time:

> The maintenance man at the Homes has found employment elsewhere, but the heating equipment is being cared for by an engineer with a chief engineer's license; the Country Store, which takes the place of the usual Gift and Coffee Shop in other homes, was re-opened; a "Shop-In" by Field-Schlick is being planned so that the ladies will not have to endure the difficulties of shopping in crowded stores downtown; and daily chapel services are being held during Lent.

On another occasion, Reverend Dodgson spoke revealingly of residents' concerns about their financial futures after monthly rental rates had been increased:

> Many of our people who have exhausted their own funds and are now on welfare assistance will have to be helped by our Emergency Aid Fund. Others who have sufficient funds for the time being are very anxious for the future and very fearful of their security. They are of the generation who abhor welfare help.

He also sought to convey to the board the peace of mind that Presbyterian Homes provided to residents:

> A couple who moved in just before the New Year look upon our Home as a haven of security and are very vocal in their depth of appreciation for it. They could no longer cope with grocery shopping and driving the car in the cold weather.

Reverend Dodgson's sensitive expressions reflect the prevailing sentiment among the administration, staff, and volunteers in the early years of that close-knit environment. Together, they worked in fellowship to promote the physical, mental, emotional, social, and spiritual well-being of residents. Custodians and beauticians were among those who touched residents' lives, the superintendent's door was always open, and secretaries and receptionists wrapped Christmas presents and mopped floors after typing letters and answering phones. Years after the fact, a dietary assistant was remembered for bringing a rose to whoever was celebrating a birthday. "There are no easy problems in the work of Presbyterian Homes," Reverend Dodgson wrote in his 1968 annual report. "It requires immense sympathy on the part of all of those connected . . . to work congenially and happily in providing services to the residents."

Doing what was needed was a core value of Presbyterian Homes, and virtually everyone subscribed to it with devotion and enthusiasm. The seeds of commitment, attitude, and dedication had been sown in the organization's first two decades. Their roots would firmly hold as the evolving needs of older adults—particularly those requiring greater skilled care in addition to housing—challenged Presbyterian Homes to embrace increasingly high-tech services while staying true to its faith-based purpose.

CHAPTER TWO

A Time to Heal

PROVIDING SKILLED CARE AND SERVICES

OF NECESSITY, the mission of Presbyterian Homes began to evolve toward providing healing as well as housing to older adults. The evolution prompted the organization to add skilled care beds at Arden Hills with the 1972 construction of the Newton Wing. Six years later, the campus built the McKnight Care Center, which provided skilled care to 208 residents. The center also offered outreach services—such as home-based health care—to older adults in the neighborhood who lived on their own but needed occasional medical attention. The demand for short-term and long-term transitional care continued to expand the organization's service repertoire and, aided by increased research and training, to raise its level of quality and sophistication in skilled care. Today, some component of health care—whether nutrition classes, assisted living, memory care, or hospice—is available to every resident through the Presbyterian Homes & Services continuum of care.

THE NEED FOR SKILLED CARE

As early as 1967, the Presbyterian Homes board began to discuss the emerging need for skilled care and dementia care and its probable effect on the organization's future. The issue had been brought to the attention of the board's Homes Advisory Committee by one of its dynamic members, Dr. B. J. Kennedy. As head of medical oncology at the University of Minnesota Medical School, Dr. Kennedy had researched and developed treatments for breast and testicular cancers. But it was his interest in cancer in the elderly that drew him to serve on the Presbyterian Homes board (becoming chair in 1984), and eventually to help the organization emerge as a leader in geriatric care.

Dr. Kennedy said that, although it seemed desirable for Presbyterian Homes to continue its retirement focus, it should also consider providing for the residents' changing needs. He urged Presbyterian Homes to upgrade operations in three areas: providing medical supervision of residents by individual family physicians; offering preventive medical care; and arranging for hospitalization and skilled care as necessary. "Presbyterian Homes must undergo continuing changes in order to meet the economic and health conditions of the era," Dr. Kennedy argued.

In 1968, superintendent Harry Dodgson expanded upon Dr. Kennedy's observations.

"The aging members of our communities are naturally concerned about what will happen to them when they become infirm of body and mind," Reverend Dodgson reported. Many residents reported that they had been promised lifetime care, but the limited size and scope of the Home made it impossible to keep that promise. At minimum, thirty to fifty more skilled care beds were needed. And it was apparent that the need for specialized care was growing among prospective newcomers to Presbyterian Homes. In that year alone, eight of twenty applicants—all well into their eighties—had been turned down for admission because they required full skilled care. Likewise, several applicants had transferred into Presbyterian Homes from nursing homes when it became apparent that they didn't need full skilled care but still required some skilled assistance.

Overall, Reverend Dodgson pointed out, the entire elder care environment had changed since the Home opened in 1955, and particularly since the Irving Adams West Wing opened in 1963. Residents were living longer and often requiring more care at greater expense; as fees rose, many retirees needed to look at less expensive accommodations. Owing largely to the expansion of government services for the elderly, subsidized housing was now available at more affordable rates. The Home's annual entrance fee in 1963 was $1,000 for Presbyterians ($2,000 for non-Presbyterians) and rental rates started at $125 per month. In 1968, room rates—already approaching $200 per month—were raised $20 on April 1, and another $35 on December 1. By comparison, federally subsidized apartments were renting at $30 to $40 a month. For the first time, Presbyterian Homes had vacancies. The realities of dealing with increasing numbers of residents who required skilled care on the one hand and with competition from the government on the other could neither be denied nor overlooked.

THE NEED TO RESTRUCTURE

Faced with these challenges, the Presbyterian Homes board sought counsel from Ellis G. Willard, executive director of Presbyterian Homes of the Synod of New Jersey. In October 1968, Willard presented a comprehensive overview of the situation and its prospective solutions. He began by describing the structure of his organization, which consisted of three complexes that together served 600 residents. Unlike its Minnesota counterpart, the New Jersey board was charged exclusively with making policy. Daily operations at each complex, including admissions, were the responsibility of its administrator. Four committees dealt with matters of planning and development, finance, public relations, and administration. The New Jersey organization also had eliminated life-care contracts, which prevented it from receiving state welfare-assistance funds.

Next, Willard addressed the benefits of government involvement in nursing homes. Medicaid and Medicare were both good for older people, he argued, despite that each program required senior care providers to follow federal standards and maintain extra recordkeeping. Nevertheless, he pointed out, "it would appear that your eighteen-bed nursing care section is economically too small to pay its own way. You should have between fifty and seventy-five beds to [break even]. If you sign up for Medicare, you would have to have extra trained staff and extra equipment, plus a physical therapy room, with a physical therapist in attendance, and this would add greatly to the cost of your operation."

Willard also advised Presbyterian Homes to make a thorough study of beds available in nearby nursing homes before deciding to build an extended care or skilled care center. "Your board will have to study what is needed most in the future of your area, and then restate your philosophy," he said. "Extended care will be increasingly required because people are living longer and their health breaks down slowly." In addition, he said, residents with dementia should not be mixed in with regular residents, but rather cared for in a separate wing or building for specialized attention.

The board agreed to adopt most of Willard's recommendations. It would become a policy-making and program development body only, transferring oversight of daily operations to the Home's superintendent. The Executive Committee would create four committees—finance, planning and development, public relations, and administration—to delineate the board's relationship to the superintendent. Presbyterian Homes would hire a physician to provide routine medical supervision of residents and would contract with hospitals and extended-care centers when necessary. The board would consider developing adult daycare and short-term care and recruiting individuals with expertise in institutional management to serve as board members. At the same time the bylaws were revised to include these changes, the Presbyterian Homes board also moved to eliminate the Home's admission fee as of January 1, 1969.

The 1969 annual report again made reference to the changing face of geriatric care, noting that a study was under way to determine the need for a new elder care building at Presbyterian Homes. "The problem," the report explained, "is whether to build for ambulatory care or for nursing care. If the new building is devoted to ambulatory care, then additional plans will have to be made for nursing home care." At a March board meeting, the Reverend James Grant discussed statistics he had compiled concerning the residents of Presbyterian Homes, including those needing hospital care and skilled care. Like Ellis Willard before him, Reverend Grant believed that Presbyterian Homes needed to double its skilled care beds before expanding its residential capacity. His research confirmed that many of the administrative problems encountered by Reverend Dodgson and his staff "could be alleviated by not having to displace residents needing nursing care to other nursing homes." Reverend Grant conceded that doubling Presbyterian Homes' skilled care beds would create staffing problems of its own. "But if the goal of any institution for aging is concerned foremost with the priorities of the health and welfare, and the dignity and comfort, of their residents," he argued, then adding skilled care beds was a high priority.

Recognizing the need for staff leadership, Reverend K. William Hagstrom was recruited in 1970 by Dr. West and Dr. B. J. Kennedy to become superintendent of Presbyterian Homes. Reverend Hagstrom had briefly worked for the organization before leaving to create the welfare department for Bloomington, Minnesota. He not only understood the far-reaching benefits of Ellis Willard's and James Grant's recommendations, he saw the critical need for a process of strategic planning. Reverend Hagstrom made both a reality. He also set to work, immediately hiring architects and contractors to build the Newton Wing at the Presbyterian Home.

NEWTON WING
ARDEN HILLS, 1972

Following his retirement from the House of Hope Presbyterian Church in 1969, Dr. Irving Adams West offered his services "with the responsibility of soliciting funds, gifts and bequests . . . to attempt to undergird the financial structure of [the Home], as well as the possibility of expanding its physical facilities." The task was precisely the one he had pursued for the better part of a quarter century. Now, free of other constraints, he moved ahead with determination. The Newton Wing was his first major achievement in that capacity.

Made possible by another generous gift from the Newton sisters, the Newton Wing opened in 1972 at the Presbyterian Home. Its significant mix of skilled care beds and residential apartments was a direct response to the advice the board had received from Ellis Willard and James Grant. In addition to thirty-one skilled care beds and twenty-nine intermediate skilled care beds, the new wing included accommodations for fifty-seven residents. It also featured the McKnight Dining Room, funded by retired 3M CEO William L. McKnight.

Reverend Hagstrom brought a powerful sense of mission to his work. He understood the role of Presbyterian Homes in the evolution of regional elder care and advocated expansion of specialized services. The implementation of an adult daycare program in 1971 and of a home-delivered meals program in 1972 created meaningful contacts with hundreds of older neighbors and their families. Home-based rehabilitative services for partially disabled individuals did likewise. The Newton Wing's emphasis on skilled care made it clear that the board was making realistic adjustments to the changing needs of older adults.

On October 2, 1972, after considerable discussion, the organization's name was changed to Presbyterian Homes of the State of Minnesota. For nearly twenty years, the board had been committed to a single site, the Presbyterian Home. Now, the board realized, the organization's name had to reflect its expansion of services beyond one site.

The courtyard at McKnight Care Center, named for William McKnight, former CEO of 3M.

McKNIGHT CARE CENTER ARDEN HILLS, 1978

By 1974, plans were under way for building a major center for geriatric care and community services at the Presbyterian Home that would bring all existing health services under one roof, including every level of care. The center would reach out with skilled care services to older adults in the northern suburbs, thus allowing them to live independently rather than in a traditional nursing home. At the same time, such outreach services demonstrated that the center was following government mandates for the development of alternatives to hospitalization and institutionalization. The center would also stimulate research and innovation in geriatric health care, a concept long promoted by Dr. B. J. Kennedy and Reverend Hagstrom.

Dr. West knew that fund-raising for the $5.45 million initiative called for an unprecedented lead gift. In 1975 he flew to Florida to call on William L. McKnight. No stranger to Presbyterian Homes, McKnight had already funded the dining room in the Newton Wing and presented a magnificent grand piano in memory of his first wife, Maude. Dr. West presented Reverend Hagstrom's model of the proposed wing and its specialized services to McKnight. After only a moment's reflection, McKnight—who pointed out that he himself would soon be eighty-eight—pledged $2 million to the project. Within a week, the board announced that the new building would be named the McKnight Care Center. Months of public and private negotiation followed, a $4 million industrial development revenue bond was approved, and the building opened on January 16, 1978. Dr. Robert Blomberg was hired as medical director, a newly created position that Dr. Kennedy had earlier recommended that Presbyterian Homes adopt.

Residents work out in the warm water therapy pool at the McKnight Care Center.

William L. McKnight died on March 4, 1978, shortly before the center was dedicated. Had he seen it, he would have recognized it as the embodiment of Reverend Hagstrom's vision of specialized services that Dr. West had presented. The center gained immediate national recognition for its innovative approach to health care services for residents and community members alike, all housed on the first floor of the four-story structure. Services included medical and dental clinics, physical and occupational therapy, an X-ray lab, and an aquatic therapy program. Visitors came from thirty states and fifteen countries to see and understand this new model of integrated service.

The center's top three floors accommodated 192 beds, graduating from intermediate to skilled care. Sixteen short-term and respite care beds provided a place of security for a parent or grandparent while a family took a vacation and a place of care midway between hospital and home. All skilled care beds formerly located in the Newton Wing were transferred to the new center and the older building was immediately remodeled into retirement rooms. The center also had an in-house television channel, a robotics

Benefactor William L. McKnight.

food-delivery system, and a sidewalk café. The overall design permitted use of the atrium as a concert hall or assembly room.

Dr. West saw the McKnight Care Center as a resource that would deal not only with the physical health of the people it served, but with their mental and spiritual health as well. "Let's say that all these people need is to have their blood pressure checked once a week or have some therapy twice a week, or they feel sick, or maybe have an emotional problem about their families or a financial or legal matter," he said in an interview with the *St. Paul Pioneer Press*. "We'll either bring them to the center or send someone from the center to see them. It's silly to institutionalize old people if they can make it at their own homes or apartments and only need a few things to keep them well and happy. And happiness and optimism is what we're all about out here."

Reverend Hagstrom agreed. "Let the people stay in their own homes or apartments and we'll come to them," he promised. "They can come to us for their medical problems [and for their] emotional and legal and human needs." He was fond of pointing out that each service provided by Presbyterian Homes was a point on a continuum. "I like to say that people who come here aren't making the last stop on the road, just one more stop," Hagstrom wrote. "And I think the McKnight Center is going a long way toward sustaining the notion among our elderly people in Arden Hills." His fledgling continuum of care concept—the opportunity to age in one place with services changing to meet needs—would soon mature into a way of life at Presbyterian Homes.

Attending the dedication of the McKnight Care Center in 1978 are (from left) Reverend K. William Hagstrom, superintendent of Presbyterian Homes; Minnesota congressman Al Quie; Dr. Irving Adams West.

DONOR PROFILE
William L. McKnight

As president and CEO of 3M, William McKnight had a penchant for making speedy decisions. His decisiveness also served Presbyterian Homes well, especially when he agreed to help fund the geriatric care center that bears his name.

Born in Dakota Territory in 1887, McKnight joined 3M in 1907 as an assistant bookkeeper after graduating from the Duluth Business University in northern Minnesota. Over the next decade, he rose to vice president of its St. Paul headquarters. Elected president in 1929, he served in that capacity for twenty years until he became chair of the board.

McKnight was named one of seven "great contributors" to American management by the American Institute of Management, and he is widely remembered as a business philosopher who encouraged employee initiative and innovation. His personal legacy remains the McKnight Foundation, which he and his wife, Maude, founded in 1953. As one of the largest family-run foundations in the nation, the charity provides grants that champion education, the arts, and the environment, among other causes.

EMPLOYEE PROFILE
Gladys Bane

Gladys Bane was a secretary at the Shoreview Baptist Church in 1970 when the Reverend K. William Hagstrom invited her to work for him as a receptionist at the Presbyterian Home. At first, the widowed mother of three turned the superintendent down. But after prayerful consideration, she took the job and found herself on a new career path. As social services coordinator she worked with Reverend Hagstrom to develop the residents council. Soon she was handling admissions. With Reverend Hagstrom's encouragement, Bane earned her license as a nursing home administrator and became the Home's assistant administrator in the late 1970s. She retired in 1985, but returned for one year—first as director of admissions at the Bloomington campus and then at the Roseville campus.

Bane, who still lives in her Shoreview home, calls the early period under Reverend Hagstrom "the golden years." "He was just wonderful, and started so many big things that are still in place," she says. "Yet he and his wife, Ethel, took time to tend to small acts of kindness for the residents. I marvel at his philosophy, which was passed on to the staff. We had joy in doing whatever we could."

Former employee Gladys Bane.

PRESBYTERIAN HOMES OF ROSEVILLE (LANGTON LAKE PLACE), 1985

In 1982, Presbyterian Homes decided to broaden its fledgling continuum of care concept by buying, renovating, and repurposing the Lake Johanna Middle School, which had closed due to enrollment decline. Located in

Architectural rendering of Langton Lake Place chapel.

Architectural rendering of Langton Lake Place courtyard.

the St. Paul suburb of Roseville, just two blocks from the Arden Hills campus, the two-story building on twenty acres near Langton Lake offered significant advantages to Presbyterian Homes, not the least of which was proximity to and a way to relieve pressure on the McKnight Care Center, which was already stretched to capacity. It was initially thought that the remodeled building could provide accommodations for independent living and assisted living for 160 older adults, and encompass myriad innovative services—short-term care, respite care, hospice, adult daycare and nightcare centers, and home health and home chore agencies. Supportive services for residents with Alzheimer's disease, some of whom would participate in clinical research through an affiliation with the University of Minnesota, would also be based at the new property. The grounds would feature a six-acre park designed especially for older adults, with fitness trails for hiking and cross-country skiing, a baseball diamond and tennis courts, picnic shelters, a gazebo, and a wildflower garden.

The projected cost of the project was $7 million, but by substantially revising the original design, the cost was reduced. In addition to delaying renovation of a swimming pool, all rental apartments were eliminated in favor of 165 skilled care beds, which would serve residents with Alzheimer's, provide long- and short-term skilled care, and offer hospice. Langton Lake Place (renamed Langton Place in 1989 and Presbyterian Homes of Roseville in 1992) opened in July 1985 when the home care agency moved in; the first residents arrived on August 11, 1986. The cornerstone reads:

Opened to serve youth, 1961.
Renewed to serve the aged, 1985.
"For everything there is a season."
Ecclesiastes 3:1

David Ross became Langton Lake Place's first administrator. Major gifts for the project included $1 million from the Robert Wood Johnson Foundation and $725,000 from the estate of Mary Schultz Gray.

DONOR PROFILE

Mary Schultz Gray

Giving was a way of life for Mary Schultz Gray, whose generous contributions have fostered many nonprofit organizations in the Twin Cities, including Presbyterian Homes.

This Minnesota farm girl attended Mankato State Teacher's College and the University of Minnesota before joining the staff at the YWCA in Dubuque, Iowa. She next accepted a counseling job with the Chicago YWCA, eventually becoming director of a dormitory for young women. After she married Ward Gray, a YMCA staff member, they moved back to Minnesota and became members of Grace Presbyterian Church (now Grace Trinity).

Through her careful investments, Mary Schultz Gray was able to support many charities, including Courage Center, Children's Home Society, and the Minneapolis Society for the Blind. After her death in 1986, several Presbyterian Homes campuses—including Boutwells Landing, EagleCrest, and Bloomington—benefited from her generous gifts.

EMPLOYEE PROFILE

Chaplain Bill Chadwick

Presbyterian Homes of Roseville provides long-term skilled care for older adults and short-term transitional care for individuals recovering from illness or surgery. Short-term care also includes hospice care. In his three years as spiritual director at Roseville, Chaplain Bill Chadwick has instituted three innovative hospice programs.

The Abiders Program matches hospice residents with volunteers who provide companionship. The Comfort Care Program distributes baskets filled with such reassuring items as a Bible, a book light,

Benefactor Mary Schultz Gray.

Morrison Gillet and resident Harriet Gillet.

music CDs, and a brightly colored quilt. The third program—"the Procession of Honor"—offers a more personal farewell to residents who have died. After family members have said their goodbyes, they accompany their loved one to the nursing station. There, they gather with residents and staff while Chadwick offers a prayer over the individual, whose body is draped in white linen decorated with a cross. The group then walks alongside the body to the waiting hearse, where Chadwick bestows a final blessing.

"We work with a lot of people in crisis," says Chadwick, a former parish pastor. "It is an honor, a sacred privilege, to be allowed into their lives at this time."

The Alzheimer's Care Center at Langton Lake Place was launched in October 1986 in collaboration with University of Minnesota psychologists and neurologists. One of the first of its kind in the United States, the center offered specialized care to residents with Alzheimer's. It also became a center for clinical research of the sort advocated years earlier by Dr. B. J. Kennedy. Previously, the only long-term care option for such individuals was a traditional nursing home. The care center's staff—all veterans of long-term care settings—were trained to be flexible and tolerant in the more relaxing and homelike environment of the new center. To help families better understand the disease, a support group was organized as well. In 1997, to better serve the needs of residents, Presbyterian Homes of Roseville focused on short- and long-term rehabilitative care as well as hospice, while residents with Alzheimer's were cared for at the McKnight Care Center and in the memory care programs at various PHS sites.

FAMILY PROFILE *Morrison Gillet*

Twice a day Morrie Gillet goes to the McKnight Care Center in Arden Hills to feed lunch and dinner to his wife, Harriet. "The staff would feed her if I weren't here, but I like to do that," Gillet explains. Harriet, who has Alzheimer's, is a resident in the McKnight Center's memory care program, which assists individuals with advanced cases of the disease. The program provides exercise classes, church services, piano music, and word games, among other activities.

As a member of the family council of Presbyterian Homes of Arden Hills, Morrie Gillet helps plan monthly dinner gatherings for relatives of people with Alzheimer's. Health care experts meet once a month with families to help them understand the disease's effects on their loved ones. Gillet has heartfelt praise for the care his wife receives, from the physician who visits her weekly to the staff who turn her every two hours to prevent bed sores. "The staff just have wonderful patience and sympathy for the afflicted," he says.

Expanding its continuum of care concept throughout the 1990s led Presbyterian Homes to add health care services in other Twin Cities suburbs and to offer training opportunities for health care professionals.

PRESBYTERIAN HOMES ON LAKE MINNETONKA SPRING PARK, 1991

Presbyterian Homes' presence in the western Twin Cities area began with its 1991 purchase of the Twin Birch Health Care Center and Lakeshore Village. Located on six acres in the Twin Cities suburb of Spring Park, the community consisted of the care center, The Residence (now The Chateau), an assisted living center, and the Villa Apartments and the Court Apartments, both rental buildings.

Renamed Presbyterian Homes on Lake Minnetonka, the community offers a full continuum of care, including skilled care, short-term and transitional care, and long-term care and memory care. Thirty-seven assisted living apartments and 160 independent living apartments overlook 800 feet of lakeshore as well as grounds that feature a fountain, three ponds, and a park whose paths accommodate

Presbyterian Homes on Lake Minnetonka in Spring Park, Minnesota.

The Spring Park grounds feature handicapped-accessible garden paths.

The Arbor at EagleCrest in Roseville, Minnesota, serves as a regional dementia training center.

Castle Ridge Manor House in Eden Prairie, Minnesota, was acquired in 2002.

wheelchairs and motorized chairs. Dental and lab services are on-site, as are adult daycare and child daycare.

THE ARBOR AT EAGLECREST ROSEVILLE, 2001

In 1997, Presbyterian Homes turned its attention to creating a dementia center within EagleCrest, a retirement campus in Roseville, Minnesota, managed by Presbyterian Homes for Northwestern College and later acquired by PHS. The organization viewed the dementia center—called The Arbor—as a continuation of its commitment to provide older adults with the highest quality of care in a setting designed to promote independence, dignity, and well-being.

Presbyterian Homes envisioned The Arbor as an ideal setting in which to apply everything it had learned about caring for older adults over the course of almost half a century, thereby strengthening its role as a leader and innovator among long-term care providers, particularly as a faith-based organization. In developing The Arbor, Presbyterian Homes staff and board members toured several Alzheimer's care centers in the nation and incorporated their most successful components into The Arbor's design. When it opened on January 3, 2001, The Arbor at EagleCrest became a regional dementia training center as well as a housing community. The center cross-trains employees using the universal-worker concept—meaning they are dietary aide, housekeeper, and personal-care worker all in one. The center also offers instruction in strategies and systems to other providers of assisted living, adult daycare, and skilled care for persons with Alzheimer's. The center extends its services to the entire community, offering training and support to caregivers and families as a premier resource for Alzheimer's research.

Launching The Arbor at EagleCrest therefore became another critical benchmark in Presbyterian Homes' goal of expanding continuum of care communities, specifically in the northern Twin Cities. It also paved the way for creating memory care centers at many of its campuses.

CASTLE RIDGE
EDEN PRAIRIE, 2002

In December 2002, the Presbyterian Homes board approved the $5 million purchase of Castle Ridge. The care center was part of a continuum of care campus built by Twin City Christian Homes. The concept was a little ahead of its time, however, and its owners had concluded that operation of a small, stand-alone skilled care center in a highly competitive health care environment was no longer feasible. Castle Ridge consists of twenty-one assisted living apartments (called The Manor House) and a sixty-bed skilled care center. Short-term care is also provided.

In the fall of 2004, Presbyterian Homes & Services also acquired The Broadmoor, a 227-unit apartment building attached to Castle Ridge. The $13 million property was leased in part to older adults, with the remaining apartments leased to the general public. The process of making The Broadmoor a community for older adults exclusively is ongoing. When that transition is complete, Castle Ridge will be converted to a full continuum of care community.

HEALTH CARE TRAINING

Meeting the specialized needs of residents at care centers within Presbyterian Homes requires ongoing employee education. Two PHS initiatives are particularly involved with employee recruitment: the international BNAR (Befriender Nursing Assistant Registered) recruitment program and International Nurse Recruitment. Two other programs—DOVE and Empira—teach staff best standards and practices for residents in all care settings.

Presbyterian Homes & Services developed the BNAR recruitment program in response to a shortage of nursing assistants, who provide direct care to residents—a vital component of health care delivery within skilled care centers and assisted living apartments. In the program, the nursing assistant's duties have been broadened to take a holistic approach to the physical, social, and spiritual needs of residents.

In developing the pilot program, which began in 1999, a PHS team worked closely with the Presbyterian Church in the African republic of Cameroon to develop a rigorous application process for college graduates committed to the mission of serving older adults; each program participant has served as an elder or minister in Presbyterian churches. Their journey to the United States has been described as a leap of faith as they leave families, homes, and friends to provide care and spiritual comfort to Presbyterian Homes residents. Once BNAR applicants arrive in the Twin Cities, their education includes both nursing assistant training and Befriender Ministry training. BNARs now work at several Presbyterian Homes campuses, where their compassionate care is often praised by residents and families alike.

International Nurse Recruitment emerged as the nursing shortage in the United States grew. A partnership opportunity developed through churches in the Philippines to bring nurses to Presbyterian Homes to provide skilled care to older residents. Prospective employees must pass nursing board exams and demonstrate English language proficiency. While International Nurse Recruitment does not solve the nursing shortage, the company does bring much-needed help to several PHS sites. Since its implementation, eighty-three nurses—many from the Philippines—have joined PHS. The goal is to recruit approximately 100 nurses a year.

The DOVE program not only prepares staff for the practical challenges they are likely to face while caring for residents with dementia, it also teaches them how to work with residents in a dignified manner. A major element of DOVE—which stands for Dementia Orientation, Values, and Education—is a nine-hour training session for every employee (from housekeepers to foodservice workers to nurses) who encounters residents requiring memory care. The staff "tries to take a holistic approach to residents suffering from dementia, to see them as whole individuals, and stresses the fact that while the individual may have forgotten, God has not forgotten the individual," says Angie Swetland, DOVE director and PHS corporate support for operations.

DOVE training manuals define the standards for evaluating residents who are new to memory care, for conducting twice-a-year memory care conferences, and for interviewing prospective employees. The staff emphasizes a resident's self-esteem through self-care and life skills, such as selecting what to wear and helping to set tables for meals. Twice a year, at required "family nights," the staff helps relatives cope with the problems that dementia raises in their relationships with their loved ones. "Family members are dealing with loss, and they may not understand Mom—Mom looks normal," Swetland says. "If a person is in a wheelchair, we don't ask them to walk. But all the time we ask people with dementia to remember." With ordinary illness and disease, she points out, therapy focuses on restoring whatever function has been lost. With dementia, the decline is progressive and cannot be reversed. "So we have different roles with these individuals—above all, treating them with dignity," she says.

Each Presbyterian Homes site runs its own DOVE program, which was introduced to PHS in 2002, and repeats the nine-hour training session regularly. Swetland, who began her career in recreational therapy, oversees programming for memory care and DOVE.

The Empira training program sets the standards of health care excellence for every PHS site. Empira educates staff about problems that are often specific to residents in assisted living and care centers, such as falls, chronic pain, and incontinence. Each topic uses indicators established by the Center for Medicare and Medicaid Services to determine quality of care. PHS invites national experts to update the staff about one specific care concern, says Beckie Conway, director of home care and PHS corporate support for clinical services. "Then we organize a clinical action team made up of people from the front lines—home health aides, housekeepers—to educate everyone else on the topic."

The Empira program was initiated in 2002 at PHS in cooperation with five other Twin Cities organizations: the Birchwood Companies, Elim Homes, Minnesota Masonic Homes, Volunteers of America, and Walker Methodist. "The results of Empira are now showing up in a higher quality of care for our residents," Conway reports. She sees Empira as a natural extension of nursing practices that were evolving when she joined Presbyterian Homes in 1980 as director of home care. Back then, nurses provided care to the elderly in their homes. The required time for each visit grew from one to two hours, then four, regardless of how much help was wanted or needed. "We began to wonder if it wouldn't be more cost effective to have the services brought to individuals in a congregate setting, such as an apartment building," Conway says. "That way, we could provide just the amount of care an individual needs. Presbyterian Homes had practiced that type of care long before it was called assisted living."

For Presbyterian Homes, developing state-of-the-art health care practices and standards at PHS campuses became a time of healing for its residents. Yet the organization also wished to give older adults more choices for independent living, preferably within a continuum of care setting, and more options for lower-income housing. Embracing broader, more diverse populations would have as great an impact on Presbyterian Homes & Services as an organization as it would on its care and services programs.

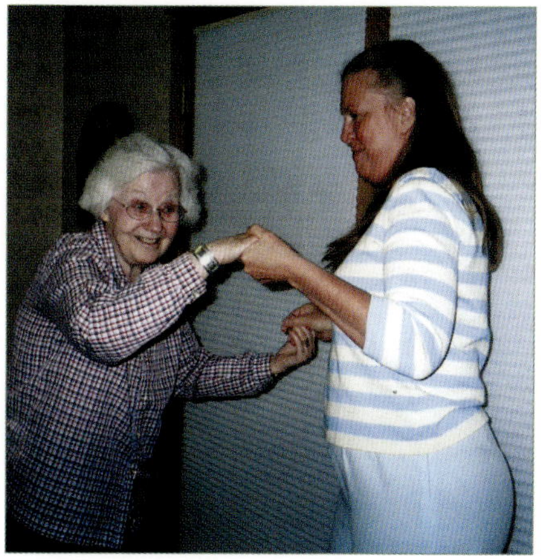

Providing residents with the highest standard of care is the goal of the Empira program.

Through DOVE, employees learn how to treat memory care residents with compassion and respect.

CHAPTER THREE

A Time to Embrace

SERVING DIVERSE NEEDS

WITH THE OPENING of the McKnight Care Center, Presbyterian Homes expanded yet again beyond its original purpose as a simple retirement community. As it added health care services to its repertoire, the organization recognized a growing demand among older adults for more options for independent living. It also felt called to embrace service to a greater cross section of older adults—those living with assistance or independently, those living in the inner city or in the suburbs, those living on limited incomes or in affluence.

Its first step in meeting the housing demand was to convert the Lake Johanna Elementary School in Arden Hills, Minnesota, into apartments suitable for couples. The next step was to pursue the revolutionary concept Reverend K. William Hagstrom had hinted at in the late 1970s: establishing independent living quarters within a continuum of care community that would allow older adults to "age in place." As necessary, residents could move from independent living quarters to assisted living apartments to skilled care centers, all under the same roof. Presbyterian Homes began to envision a "hub-and-spoke" approach to building such housing in the Twin Cities. Each quadrant of the metro area would have a hub—a full continuum of care campus consisting of independent or congregate living, assisted living, a skilled care center, and home care services, all designed to meet the specific needs of the geographic region it served. The spokes represented other choices in housing options, also tailored to serve the needs of older adults within the defined market area. The idea would eventually take hold in Wisconsin and Iowa as well.

At the same time it was creating more options for independent living, Presbyterian Homes reaffirmed its commitment to serving lower-income older adults. In offering affordable housing to a more diverse population, Presbyterian Homes also saw the advantages of managing rather than owning certain properties, and of working with the federal government on properties subsidized by the Department of Housing and Urban Development.

SUTTON PLACE
ARDEN HILLS, 1980

Lake Johanna Elementary School in Arden Hills was a simple, two-story structure on five-and-a-half acres next to the original Presbyterian Home campus. Built in 1849, then replaced and dedicated in 1939, the school was being sold in March 1978 by Mounds View School District due to enrollment decline. In the schoolhouse, Presbyterian Homes saw its chance to develop a new kind of retirement community, one that catered to older couples living independently. Dr. Irving Adams West set about looking for a donor to back the new apartment complex. After months of discussion with Dr. West, Harry Sutton—a ninety-seven-year-old resident of the Home—donated $300,000 for the project. The building was named Sutton Place in recognition of his generosity.

The old school's modular classrooms required only minor alterations to be remodeled into seventeen one-bedroom apartments and two multipurpose areas. The rest of the interior needed extensive alterations. The cost of renovation was estimated at $530,000. When the first bids arrived, however, the lowest came in at $1.1 million. If the board seriously considered retreating, there is no evidence of it. It approved a budget of $1.3 million to complete the project as a nineteen-unit structure, redesigned with two apartments replacing each multipurpose room. The building opened in January 1980.

Lake Johanna Middle School was transformed into Langton Lake Place in Arden Hills, Minnesota.

Lake Johanna Elementary School became Sutton Place in Arden Hills.

EMPLOYEE PROFILE
Pam Lemke

Pam Lemke has been a part of Presbyterian Homes of Arden Hills since 1958,

Resident, volunteer, and former employee Pam Lemke with Arden Hills activities director Nancy Johnson.

when a summer job led to a forty-seven-year career. In that time, Lemke did a little of everything, from wrapping gifts to collecting rent. She sorted and delivered mail, mopped the halls, and did the payroll. She took residents to their appointments and wrote their notes of thanks to friends and family. Every other weekend, when she stayed overnight at the Home, "I would check all of them and bid them good night," she recalls. Lemke even created a charting system for the residents, using stenography tablets to record their health care information. "I loved every day of it," she says. "I have been a caregiver from the day I was born."

Lemke herself now lives on the Arden Hills campus in Sutton Place in an apartment that was once her son's classroom before the building was converted from a school into apartments. Her dining room was once the school cafeteria where she served hot lunches and her Cub Scout troop met. She now spends almost every day volunteering as a chapel usher and visiting residents. "I wouldn't want to quit," she says.

The decision to buy and convert Lake Johanna Elementary School into apartments was a turning point in the evolution of Presbyterian Homes. Occasionally a wife and husband would move into the Home, but the majority of residents were women living alone. Of the individuals living at the Home in 1974, there were thirteen married couples, plus thirty men and and 117 women. Moreover, those residents in 1974 were older on average than those of the late 1950s and early 1960s—in 1974 the average age of residents was 84.6—and they often had health problems that required specialized attention. At that time, "independent living" did not mean "apartment living"; it meant only that skilled care was not needed. Few of the rooms at the Home were large enough to be attractive to most couples anyway. Nor had the Home specifically solicited an apartment clientele. The availability of Lake Johanna Elementary School allowed Presbyterian Homes to do that.

Dr. West understood that by creating Sutton Place, Presbyterian Homes could meaningfully respond to the rapidly expanding needs of older individuals, including some who were younger than sixty-five. The consequences of his vision are obvious in the independent living options presently available to individuals and couples throughout Presbyterian Homes & Services, from townhomes to two- and three-bedroom apartments. Sutton Place, the first Presbyterian Homes independent living community, was followed by PHS independent living communities in Bloomington and elsewhere.

PRESBYTERIAN HOMES OF BLOOMINGTON (GIDEON POND CENTER), 1985

As it was pursuing the Langton Lake Place project, Presbyterian Homes was approached by Christ Presbyterian Church, located in the Minneapolis suburb of Edina, about partnership in and development of a full-service retirement community known as Gideon Pond Center.

The project's history is long and complex. In the early 1970s, under the leadership of Reverend Roger Anderson, Christ Presbyterian Church began to look into building a retirement community on its property. "I felt we needed a first-class home for older adults in the southwest part of the metropolitan area," said Reverend Anderson, "and we wanted to do it right." Church members Robert and Betty Pond led Christ Presbyterian in pursuing the project and contributed to the effort. By 1976, an architect had drawn preliminary plans for a retirement home that would be connected to the church so that residents could participate in the life of the congregation and so that the congregation could minister to the elderly. The project would consist exclusively of independent living apartments.

When the land that Christ Presbyterian Church had designated for the building was taken by the state for developing a highway, progress on the project came to a standstill. In 1981, the committee—led by Reverend Harry Maghakian of Valley Presbyterian Church—recommended that the Presbytery itself take on the project. In 1982, when a study by the city of Bloomington showed a need for additional low- to moderate-cost housing and support services for older adults, the Synod of Lakes and Prairies went into action. The Synod, under whose auspices Presbyterian Homes operates, invited the organization to sponsor the project and share its expertise, but the Presbyterian Homes board decided to limit its involvement to staff resources. Plans for Gideon Pond Center moved ahead without equity investment from Presbyterian Homes, and a joint venture was formed with the Bloomington Development Committee, with completion projected for 1990. The project's name honored Gideon Hollister Pond, a Presbyterian missionary who came to the Minnesota Territory in 1834.

HISTORY PROFILE
Gideon Hollister Pond

The first building within Presbyterian Homes of Bloomington bears the name of Reverend Gideon Hollister Pond, whose commitment to Christian missions in Minnesota provided inspiration for the development.

In 1831 in Washington, Connecticut, Pond dedicated himself to missionary

Missionary Gideon Hollister Pond.

Missionary Samuel Pond.

Architectural rendering of Gideon Pond housing.

work. He was twenty-four years old when he and his older brother, Samuel, landed at Minnesota's Fort Snelling in 1834. Reverend William Thurston Boutwell was among those who greeted the young missionaries on their arrival. Sent to work among the Dakota people, the Pond brothers were the first settlers in what became Minnesota's Hennepin County. The cabin they built near Lake Calhoun was the first chapel, first school, and first mission station for the Dakotas. The brothers learned the Dakota language and created a written alphabet that is still in use.

After several moves, Gideon Pond, his wife, and their growing family settled in the Minnesota River Valley in what is now the city of Bloomington. He continued to teach Dakota and settler children, and started the Oak Grove mission, which in 1855 became Oak Grove Presbyterian Church. When he died in 1878, his wife noted that as "Mr. Pond lay in his coffin here in our home, the Indians flocked to see his dead body and as they gazed their tears dripped to the floor and they said, 'We have lost one of our best friends.'"

Gideon Pond Center had a distinctive personality. It was designed in part as a cooperative for more active older adults who wished to own rather than lease, and in part as rental housing for low-income elderly that was subsidized through the Department of Housing and Urban Development. Phase I of the development was called The Residence at Gideon Pond; it was a forty-five-unit building, subsidized by HUD 202/Section 8, that opened in May 1985. (Phase I was renamed Newton Manor in 1988.) Phase II, a 101-unit cooperative called Gideon Pond, opened in February 1987, with each owner of co-op shares receiving an exclusive lease to occupy a particular apartment. Phase III, named The Gardens, was slated to open in 1992 as an eighty-unit assisted living building with additional space devoted to community-based health care services. Phase IV would later become a skilled care center, although ground would not be broken for the project for more than twenty years after it was envisioned as part of the larger Gideon Pond campus.

Gideon Pond Center faced a set of financial problems as unique as its personality. In 1984, just as construction was getting under way, the Minnesota Legislature imposed a moratorium on increasing the number of nursing home beds in the state, making it necessary for Gideon Pond Center to reconsider its four construction phases, particularly the skilled care center. Sales of cooperative apartments also lagged behind projections, making it unlikely that the Phase II construction loan would be paid off as scheduled and even more unlikely that all 101 apartments would be sold by the projected date of August 1988. Slow sales were compounded by a glut of housing for older adults in the Twin Cities; 2,200 apartments for older adults had been added to the metro-area market between the building of Phase I and II of Gideon Pond Center. In addition, under terms of the overall plan, construction on the Phase III assisted living building could not begin until commitments had been received for 90 percent of the Phase II cooperative apartments. The Synod of Lakes and Prairies recognized the difficult circumstances that the center was in and turned to Presbyterian Homes for help. The board reluctantly agreed to take on the challenge of turning the project around, and made it an organizational priority to the exclusion of all other initiatives.

It appeared that the joint venture might have to borrow on its line of credit unless the construction loan was refinanced. In January 1988, Presbyterian Homes voted to restructure debt on Phase II through internal financing. It bought out the balance of Phase II apartments and worked with the contractor to reduce existing debts and defer payments on the rest. In June 1989, Presbyterian Homes decided to dissolve the development arrangement, taking full title to the balance of the property. By the fall of 1992, construction on

Ridgeview Terrace opened in 1991 in Bloomington, Minnesota.

the assisted living building known as The Gardens had begun.

By 1993, Gideon Pond Center had not attained full occupancy from sales, and chief financial officer Dan Lindh recommended to the Executive Committee of Presbyterian Homes that the Phase II cooperative be converted to a rental model. The apartments were fully occupied only because generous board members and others had gradually purchased one-third of the apartments and rented them at moderate prices. Presbyterian Homes had invested about $5.1 million in the development; a more aggressive buyout plan was now deemed essential. It would take another $2 million to complete the buyout, but by May 1993 the Executive Committee was able to report that, for the first time in its history, Gideon Pond Center had operated in the black.

RIDGEVIEW TERRACE BLOOMINGTON, 1991

In early 1989, when the Gideon Pond Center financial situation had begun to stabilize but before the joint venture was dissolved, the city of Bloomington asked Presbyterian Homes to consider building a separate, eighty-unit HUD-subsidized complex. Initially called the Rich Road Senior Housing Project, then briefly renamed Gideon Pond West and eventually Ridgeview Terrace, the complex was to be located just two miles from the Gideon Pond campus. By October, Presbyterian Homes CEO Daniel Bolhouse, who in 1986 had succeeded Reverend Hagstrom, reported that a HUD 202/Section 8 application for a smaller, fifty-one-unit housing project had been approved. Bloomington and HUD officials agreed that the project could move forward.

The Gideon Pond Phase III Committee gave the Presbyterian Homes board five reasons to move ahead with the HUD project: First, it fit Presbyterian Homes' mission. Second, it would help expand the mission of serving the less affluent. Third, additional housing for older adults within a six-mile radius could increase the chances of securing more beds for the Phase IV skilled care center, a top priority in Presbyterian Homes' Strategic Long Range Plan. Fourth, additional subsidized housing in Bloomington was virtually guaranteed to succeed because of strong market demand. And fifth, the management fee generated by the HUD project would ease the financial burden on Langton Place and the Presbyterian Home to support overall management services.

Initially approved as a four-story structure, Ridgeview Terrace was modified to three stories to accommodate concerns of neighboring homeowners. The building opened on June 1, 1991.

RESTRUCTURING PRESBYTERIAN HOMES

The period during which Langton Lake Place and Gideon Pond Center emerged also saw the reorganization of Presbyterian Homes. With the likelihood of additional campuses and services appearing on the horizon, the board realized that a change in its corporate structure was advisable. A parent corporation, to be known as the Presbyterian Homes of Minnesota, was created to administer and develop programs through Johanna Shores (Presbyterian Homes of Arden Hills), Langton Lake Place (Presbyterian Homes of Roseville), and Gideon Pond Center (Presbyterian Homes of Bloomington). On June 29, 1984, the Council of the Synod of Lakes and Prairies approved the revised articles of incorporation and bylaws.

To lead these new entities, Craig W. Freeman, M.D., was elected chair of the Arden Hills board, Barbara O'Grady became chair of the Roseville board, and Veryl Nyberg continued as chair of the Bloomington board. Staff changes also followed this move to a corporate model of governance. In 1984 Reverend Hagstrom was named first president and CEO of Presbyterian Homes. Dan Bolhouse, an experienced long-term care administrator, was recruited as administrator at Arden Hills. When Reverend Hagstrom retired in 1986, Bolhouse succeeded him. Chief financial officer Dan Lindh became chief operating officer.

Under Bolhouse, strategic planning and the corporate model of governance became well established. He emphasized building "customer" relations, regularly visiting each campus and its residents and staff. Bolhouse also believed that the work of Presbyterian Homes was a ministry, and emphasized the importance of seeking the Lord's guidance in each opportunity for growth. Fund-raising expanded as well, with continuing assistance from Dr. West, by then an emeritus board member and Arden Hills resident. His commitment to promoting Presbyterian Homes grew with each new project, which, he observed, combined lofty goals with practicality. "We have not only had our dreams," he said, "but we have made reality a focal point."

STRATEGIC LONG RANGE PLANNING

During the challenging time of turning Gideon Pond Center around, significant staff and board time was committed to changes that needed to be made to the Bloomington project. A question asked during that time was, "If the same kind of time and attention could be devoted in the future, what might be the result?" In response, a Strategic Long Range Plan was created.

Motivated by a desire to excel as it expanded, Presbyterian Homes developed a Strategic Long Range Planning Committee in 1989, chaired by Curt Fritze. Planning had always been part of Fritze's approach to organizational issues as an executive with the Control Data Corporation, and he was determined to get his Presbyterian Homes colleagues thinking along the same lines. Later that year, Barry Knight of Merrill Lynch headed the committee at a watershed point. Although Presbyterian Homes had long promoted a continuum of care concept, it was obvious to Knight that multiple opportunities existed for the expansion of elder care services throughout the Twin Cities metro area. So Knight, chief financial officer Dan Lindh, board chair Don Garretson, and future board chair Hugh Schilling began to develop the organization's first Strategic Long Range Plan.

In January 1990, the Strategic Long Range Planning Committee presented recommendations for the plan to the board. After studying the senior health care industry nationally and locally to decide how best to position Presbyterian Homes, the committee saw that future leadership in the industry would not be defined by size alone, but also by quality and innovation. Over the next forty years, a social rather than medical model would dictate how care would be delivered. Alternative care delivery systems would expand, continuum of care communities would remain in high demand, and an increasing need for subacute care services would emerge. Consumer preference would drive customization of services, which were likely to be provided through a single provider to streamline the continuum of care as an individual's needs changed. Medicare and Medicaid reimbursement would remain erratic because government at all levels would continue to have difficulty in balancing budgets. The greatest demand would be for low and moderately priced housing; and in general the biggest opportunity would be housing and housing services. Echoing the 1968 cautions of consultant Ellis Willard, the committee's report also said that Presbyterian Homes was operating at a size that was inefficient and costly. It needed a larger base of skilled care beds (there were 373) and an increased number of assisted living and independent living apartments to operate efficiently. The organization had to grow or downsize, and in the committee's view, growth was the only option.

Growth meant completing the development of a four-campus "hub and spoke" system in the Twin Cities metropolitan area. Each of four continuum of care centers would be centrally located within the region it served—an area within a six-mile radius—and would be designed specifically for the needs of that area to achieve greatest efficiency and effectiveness. In 1990, the northern hub consisted of the Arden Hills and Roseville campuses; the Bloomington campus was the hub in the south. The Strategic Long Range Planning Committee suggested that the third continuum of care hub be developed in the western suburbs for reasons of demographics, service needs, and the potential donor base. Additional hubs could follow, with emphasis on the eastern suburbs and otherwise underserved areas.

The Strategic Long Range Plan adopted in 1991 thus defined a clear path for Presbyterian Homes to follow. It was the beginning of an explosive period of growth and development that has continued to the present.

THE MAYFIELD LITTLE CANADA, 1993

The Mayfield development in Little Canada, a suburb of St. Paul, was Presbyterian Homes' first initiative into a housing-only community. In early 1991, officials in Little Canada were in need of an experienced provider as a partner, and approached Presbyterian Homes with a request to help the city develop the moderate-rate independent living project for older adults. With financial commitments from Presbyterian Homes and Little Canada, the Presbyterian Homes board agreed in July 1992 to move forward

The Mayfield in Little Canada, Minnesota, was the first Presbyterian Homes site to offer housing only.

on The Mayfield. The total cost was estimated at $5.1 million.

The Mayfield opened in May 1993. The ninety-three-unit complex features an outdoor courtyard, award-winning gardens, a gazebo, and walking paths. Indoors, a library, chapel, and gift shop add a touch of small-town living. The building is a short walk away from restaurants and stores, while metro transit buses stop at the front door.

EAGLECREST ROSEVILLE, 1994

Nearly a decade before it opened its Alzheimer's care residence at EagleCrest in Roseville, Presbyterian Homes helped develop the community at the request of Northwestern College. The Roseville-based college had decided to develop the assisted living and independent living community in concert with building a motel and refurbishing an apartment building as student housing on the same site. In January 1993, Northwestern asked Presbyterian Homes to become its partner in developing, marketing, and managing the $21 million project, which included demolition of a former motel on the property, Paul's Place. The partnership began in 1994.

EagleCrest Commons is part of the larger EagleCrest campus in Roseville, Minnesota.

The partnership offer came at an opportune time for Presbyterian Homes. Since 1991, one of the goals of its Strategic Long Range Plan had been to seek up to five management contracts with other senior care organizations in the metropolitan area. The contract with the college benefited both partners as it created new referrals between EagleCrest and Presbyterian Homes' Arden Hills and Roseville campuses. The contract also allowed Presbyterian Homes to fully employ its accounting and personnel resources without limiting or tapping resources that could or should be used for other types of development. And through involvement in the EagleCrest project and use of the revenue it generated, Presbyterian Homes could support other projects.

The partnership between College Properties, a Northwestern College subsidiary, and Presbyterian Homes led to the management of 127 independent living apartments and ninety-one assisted living apartments, plus a fifty-seven-room Country Inn and Suites Motel. By April 1998, the opportunity presented itself to restructure College Properties and EagleCrest on favorable terms. By December, Presbyterian Homes acquired College Properties for $300,000 and an assumption of a $5.6 million guarantee. Six months later, Presbyterian Homes approved expansion of the motel, which had the highest occupancy of any licensed Country Suites property in North America. The renovation, including a restaurant addition, was completed in 2000, followed in 2001 by the Alzheimer's residence known as The Arbor.

PARTNER PROFILE

Northwestern College

Presbyterian Homes' EagleCrest campus in Roseville, Minnesota, might never have existed if not for Don Ericksen, president of Northwestern College. In 1977, Ericksen (then dean of students) needed better housing for his students and had his eye on an apartment complex nearby. At first the owner declined to sell, but by 1990 the apartment building and its fourteen acres belonged to Northwestern.

Ericksen was well acquainted with Presbyterian Homes—his mother-in-law, Clara Fenton, lived at the Arden Hills residence—so he asked the organization to manage EagleCrest. "There was never anything but good in our partnership with Presbyterian Homes," Ericksen says.

By 1998, Northwestern had sold the EagleCrest complex to Presbyterian Homes, although the synergy between the two organizations continues. Students still find employment at EagleCrest while residents attend lectures and concerts at Northwestern. Students enrolled in the Early Childhood Development curriculum do their practicums at a child care center run by Northwestern and located within EagleCrest. As for the apartment house that inspired the original negotiation, it is much remodeled and still the students' first choice of residence.

CENTRAL TOWERS ST. PAUL, 1998

A second major development in the mid-1990s led Presbyterian Homes in an entirely new direction. As discussions on The Mayfield project in Little Canada were taking place, the Strategic Long Range Planning Committee saw a new way to serve the poor. The Presbyterian Homes board determined that 33 percent of all services would be for income-qualified residents and 10 percent for very low income residents, with 2 percent of total revenue targeted for the Mission Benevolence Fund. Next, the

Central Towers, St. Paul, Minnesota.

board addressed the issue of whether Presbyterian Homes should be involved in the inner city. The answer was yes, if one could use The Mayfield in Little Canada as a point of reference. The St. Paul suburb certainly wasn't the inner city, but the project *was* a moderate-income, stand-alone building that could be modeled for application elsewhere. Presbyterian Homes remained open to future inner-city efforts, provided that foundations and other organizations would be committed to helping fund them.

In February 1995, almost two years after The Mayfield's completion, the board of Central Towers, a low-income apartment complex in downtown St. Paul, approached Presbyterian Homes for assistance and a possible affiliation. The nearby Central Presbyterian Church, which owned Central Towers, was in financial trouble—not only because of its commitment to the apartment complex but also because its own building, an 1887 Romanesque structure, was expensive to maintain. Its aging and dwindling congregation could no longer financially support both the church and the apartment building.

Central Towers had its own troubles. Built in 1966 to serve low-income adults, the 274-unit building was suffering from low occupancy rates and conflicts within a population that had become a mix of both younger and older residents. The community also lacked handicapped accessibility and home health care. Because of its longstanding commitment to social activism, Central Presbyterian wanted assurance that a new owner would preserve that commitment.

In April 1995, Presbyterian Homes proceeded with the affiliation, handling fund-raising as well as marketing and strategic planning. Initially it planned to combine 100 of the 274 efficiency apartments into fifty one-bedroom handicapped-accessible apartments and reposition the building to again serve older adults only. The conversion would cost about \$2 million. By July 1996, however, only \$1.67 million had been raised. Facing the prospect of a lengthy capital campaign, the board pursued a general partnership to raise cash and requested tax credits from the city of St. Paul and the Minnesota Housing Finance Authority.

Meanwhile, the scope of the project had changed considerably. Instead of doubling the size of 100 apartments, the entire building would be renovated, making 197 handicapped-accessible apartments available. The estimated cost was now \$7.5 million. Then, in an unprecedented move, HUD agreed to set aside some of its regulations to allow tax credits and Section 8 housing codes to be combined and thus make the necessary funds available. Presbyterian Homes Housing and Assisted Living became the general partner of the Central Towers Corporation, and the renovated building reopened in 1998.

For Presbyterian Homes, Central Towers was its first full encounter with a much different demographic: almost two-thirds of the renovated building's occupants had incomes of less than $7,600 per year. Conceptually and financially, the project's implications reached well beyond the organization's involvement with the renovation. "Presbyterian Homes considers this a major event," CEO Dan Lindh observed, "and HUD and other providers will repeat the model in other locations."

RESIDENT PROFILE
Lois McLaughlin

Lois McLaughlin has lived at Central Towers in downtown St. Paul since 1978, when she moved in to be near to her mother. "My mother, Emma Borees, lived on the seventh floor and called it her 'seventh Heaven,'" McLaughlin says. "She loved it here, and so do I."

When Presbyterian Homes & Services purchased Central Towers and added an exercise room, prayer services, and other improvements, McLaughlin was tickled. As a former piano teacher, she's added a few improvements of her own, including monthly sing-alongs and performances by the choir she organized.

McLaughlin is also a busy downtown volunteer, doing clerical work at the Science Museum of Minnesota (where she was a box-office employee for ten years) and at St. Joseph's Hospital. She's also the receptionist at the senior center in Galtier Plaza and collates the Sunday bulletins for her church. Oh, and one more thing: McLaughlin belongs to the Lois Club, an international organization founded in St. Paul by a group of women named—what else?—Lois.

REVISITING STRATEGIC GOALS

By the time it had affiliated with Central Towers, more than four years had passed since Presbyterian Homes had adopted its 1991 Strategic Long Range Plan. During that time, the organization had made considerable progress toward its goals. It had doubled the number of older adults it served annually, to 3,070. It had added 770 apartments to the 716 that existed in 1991 and made significant capital improvements, most notably at the Arden Hills campus and by building a new community—Beacon Hill—in Minnetonka. It had completed $60 million in new developments. It had added 720 employees and 415 volunteers. The number of older adults assisted annually through the campus Community Services division had grown from 220 to 535.

Resident Lois McLaughlin.

Presbyterian Homes also introduced standardized name changes in 1992 to eliminate marketing and identification confusion. The Presbyterian Home/Johanna Shores thus became Presbyterian Homes of Arden Hills, Langton Place became Presbyterian Homes of Roseville, Gideon Pond Center became Presbyterian Homes of Bloomington, and the Spring Park properties became Presbyterian Homes on Lake Minnetonka. Marketing issues were also addressed through a church relations position established in 1993 and a staff training program that was nearing completion.

The most important goals to be addressed in 1993 were completing moderate- and market-rate housing at existing hubs and at managed-only buildings; establishing an eastern hub; achieving better use of skilled care beds; designing and implementing the Alzheimer's/dementia assisted living apartments at The Arbor at EagleCrest; and continuing to update older buildings in Arden Hills, Bloomington, and Spring Park. Also requiring attention were such administrative details as moving management offices to a single location and developing management contracts for housing and long-term care.

Last but not least, $900,000 in contributions needed to be raised in 1995 to address smaller projects, such as repairing the heating systems at Arden Hills and Roseville and purchasing a van for Bloomington. Improvements also included installing whirlpool tubs, adding music therapy programs, and establishing family councils to facilitate interaction between staff and families of residents. Fund-raising contributions would also improve spiritual care for residents and build relations with churches, as well as enhance the Mission Benevolence Fund.

Improving spiritual care was at the heart of Presbyterian Homes' pledge that, in caring for older adults, the emphasis would be "on innovation and leadership in providing compassionate and highly competent care with the inspiration of God's love and word." Through the spiritual care program, chaplains and staff at each Presbyterian Homes community customize care plans for residents with special needs. Chaplains counsel residents and families, conduct services and study groups, and respond to requests for emotional support. Chaplains also mentor seminarians on various aspects of geriatric care so they might better serve the growing numbers of older adults in their own congregations.

Increasing the Mission Benevolence Fund allowed Presbyterian Homes to keep its vow to "promote independence, dignity, and well-being" across a broad spectrum of care as its residents grew older. The fund supported Dr. Irving Adams West's earliest notion of guaranteed perpetual care, a concept that germinated even before the Arden Hills campus opened in 1955. Back then, if their savings ran out, residents would pay what they could and the fund would pick up the rest. By 1995, the fund was spending more than $1,000 per day to assist 100 residents and home health care clients, despite attempts to keep costs down while maintaining high-quality care. Demands on the fund increased as some residents faced unexpected costs due to catastrophic illness or pension loss, or the need for two levels of care, such as independent living for one spouse and memory care for the other.

Women, who make up 80 percent of residents at Presbyterian Homes, rely on the fund most. They are more likely than men to experience financial difficulties in their later years due to longer life expectancy, lower lifetime earnings, and smaller pension income. To meet increasing demands, and to maintain 40 percent of the apartments at Minnetonka's new Beacon Hill as affordable for older adults with lower incomes, the Mission Benevolence Fund had a goal of raising $400,000.

Dr. Irving Adams West would not live to see the fund—and services to lower-income older adults—grow to exceed even his expectations. He died on February 4, 1993.

The assumptions on which the Strategic Long Range Planning Committee based its 1991 assessment remained valid in 1995 as the plan was updated. The first assumption remained the most important: that leadership in the industry would result from quality of care and innovation, not size or scope of operation. The greatest opportunity for Presbyterian Homes to make an impact in its forty years of serving older adults would be in the area of Alzheimer's and dementia care. Individuals requiring memory care represented the fastest-growing group of older adults. It was also the least-served group in terms of innovative specialized care.

Meanwhile, with development of its western hub under way, Presbyterian Homes welcomed opportunities that would significantly broaden its mission. Its expansion into Bloomington and its success in Arden Hills and Roseville had for the first time attracted the attention of other providers in the burgeoning field of elder care. The organization now found itself expanding rapidly in the Twin Cities area, which positioned it to enter into management contracts and mutually beneficial partnerships with numerous organizations, including those in Iowa and Wisconsin. A new era—a time in which to build up—had begun.

CHAPTER FOUR

A Time to Build Up

EXPANDING IN MINNESOTA AND BEYOND

BETWEEN 1995 AND 2000, Presbyterian Homes experienced a time of dynamic growth. The five years were arguably the organization's busiest, particularly after 1997, when Dan Lindh became CEO and president. One project—Mill Pond in Ankeny, Iowa—represented the organization's first foray into out-of-state ownership. Other projects, like Echo Ridge in Oakdale, were complexes that Presbyterian Homes managed first and purchased later. Each of these properties gave the organization an even stronger foothold in serving older adults. Collectively, the sites strengthened its reputation as a leader in nonprofit elder care.

Beacon Hill in Minnetonka, Minnesota.

Recognizing changes in demographics and their related opportunities, Presbyterian Homes amended its Strategic Long Range Plan and in 1997 formalized a development arm called Senior Housing Partners. Implementing this strategy positioned Presbyterian Homes to become more effective in expanding its ministry to older adults. Senior Housing Partners became primarily responsible for the development and marketing of new projects.

BEACON HILL MINNETONKA, 1995

Pleased with the outcome of the Spring Park acquisitions and impressed by the resolution of the financial issues in Bloomington, the city of Minnetonka proposed a partnership in 1993 similar to the one Presbyterian Homes had with The Mayfield in Little Canada. Confident that the latter project was working well and eager to solidify its market position in the western suburbs of the Twin

Cities, Presbyterian Homes submitted a proposal to the city of Minnetonka for an eighty-unit building in the Glen Lake neighborhood, contingent on securing $1.7 million in assistance and completing land acquisition at a site on Beacon Hill Road. The prospective project, while located eleven miles from the Spring Park campus, would be considered an addition to that hub.

By August, the city of Minnetonka agreed to secure the wooded Beacon Hill land. The Presbyterian Homes board approved construction of 110 independent living apartments and forty-two assisted living apartments, all financed with cash from Presbyterian Homes, bonds and tax increment financing from the city of Minnetonka, a block grant from Hennepin County, and a no-interest loan from the Greater Minneapolis Metropolitan Housing Corporation. The $12.5 million project was completed in the spring of 1995.

ECHO RIDGE
OAKDALE, 1995

In 1995, Presbyterian Homes agreed to a ten-year contract to manage Echo Ridge, a 100-unit moderate-rate housing complex developed by Ark Development in the St. Paul suburb of Oakdale. Echo Ridge and similar projects were part of Presbyterian Homes' strategy to develop housing where long-term opportunity and growth existed, and with little or no up-front investment. Once such projects were operating well, had a real or prospective connection to an existing or developing hub, and showed a positive cash flow, they were purchased with majority equity, usually at an increased value as supported by an appraisal. It was a strategy that enabled the organization to meet strategic objectives while minimizing startup costs. Given Echo Ridge's strategic location in the east metro market area, Presbyterian Homes acquired the $7.7 million community in 1999.

Echo Ridge in Oakdale, Minnesota.

MISSISSIPPI SHORES
MONTICELLO, 1996

Presbyterian Homes became involved with a Wedum Foundation property in 1996 when it agreed to manage Mississippi Shores, a

Mississippi Shores, Monticello, Minnesota.

Oak Crest, Spring Lake Park, Minnesota.

forty-nine-unit independent living building in Monticello, north of the Twin Cities. With its secluded wooded location on the banks of the Mississippi River, the enterprise filled quickly. Presbyterian Homes acquired the $3.8 million property in 2002.

OAK CREST SPRING LAKE PARK, 1997

Presbyterian Homes signed a second management contract in 1996, this time with Oak Crest, a 111-unit independent living community owned by Ark Development and located in the northern Twin Cities suburb of Spring Lake Park. Presbyterian Homes agreed to manage and market the building, which opened in the summer of 1997, for twelve years. Six years into the twelve-year contract, Presbyterian Homes acquired the $11.2 million property in February 2003.

MILL POND ANKENY, IOWA, 1998

In 1998, Dee and Rod Lein asked Presbyterian Homes to manage their Mill Pond Retirement Community in Ankeny, Iowa. The couple had built the complex three years earlier, starting with assisted living apartments; independent living apartments were added in 1998. By 1999, when the Leins themselves were ready to retire, they sold the $4.7 million campus to PHS to ensure that the high quality of service for residents would remain in place. Complete with walking trails and waterfalls, the Mill Pond Retirement Community sits on twenty wooded acres in Polk County. The campus now includes transitional skilled care, a health center, and a chapel. This small continuum of care complex proved that, with a proper feasibility study as a guide and with the right administrative model in place, Presbyterian Homes could successfully own remote properties in other states.

SUMMERHOUSE OF BLOOMINGTON (OXBORO), 1999

In 1997 a new approach to housing for older adults arose in Bloomington with the Oxboro Project. In 1996, while reviewing its Strategic Long Range Plan, Presbyterian Homes identified the goal of complying with development parameters proposed by the Metropolitan Council. The council had expressed concern about urban sprawl and a desire to see denser development. One area it specifically targeted was using "airspace" above commercial areas for housing. This would not only meet the needs of older adults in first- and second-ring suburban communities, it would also bring affordable homes onto the market as their older owners moved to new housing developments nearby.

Envisioned was Oxboro, an eighty-eight-unit project in a community where Presbyterian Homes was committed to projecting a strong presence. The board voted to proceed with construction of Oxboro, to be known as SummerHouse of Bloomington. Commercial space and housing for older adults in the $10.9 million development opened in 1999. In addition to addressing urban sprawl, the project was important in more fully developing the southern suburbs' continuum of care and services.

Mill Pond in Ankeny, Iowa.

BLOOMINGTON CARE CENTER (EAGLE NURSING HOME), 1997

The continuum of care issue was partially addressed in April 1996, when Presbyterian Homes' Executive Committee approved acquisition of the Eagle Nursing Home, an eighty-bed care center just two miles from Gideon Pond. The thirty-year-old building was far from state-of-the-art but in good condition. Most important, it would provide state-licensed Medicare- and Medicaid-certified skilled care beds transferable to the Bloomington campus as it became fully developed. The purchase was completed on March 1, 1997. Eagle Nursing Home was renamed Presbyterian Homes Bloomington Care Center, with the assumption that it would continue to provide support services to the Bloomington campus for three to seven years. By then, a new care center on the campus would take its place and beds relocated to that site.

THE FARMSTEAD AT ANDOVER, 1998

The Farmstead at Andover—a $13.8 million, 140-unit mini-continuum of care community—is similar to but slightly smaller than the Beacon Hill project in Minnetonka. Presbyterian Homes developed The Farmstead property in 1998, and it became its own not-for-profit corporation in 2003. The complex consists of sixty-six independent living apartments, sixty-eight assisted living apartments, and six cottages. A red round barn, built in the 1880s and one of two such architectural novelties in Anoka County, Minnesota, is the centerpiece of the campus.

Little is known about the early origins of The Farmstead property. Swiss immigrants John and Margaret Bass bought the land in 1926

The round barn at The Farmstead.

and raised dairy cattle there for a year. Ownership turned over at least twice before George and Maja Adolfson bought it in 1950. George had grown up on a farm in Sweden; after immigrating to the United States and working for a large construction company, he started his own business called George the Builder. In 1946 he and Gordon Peterson became partners in the firm that still bears their names. Financially secure and dreaming of living again on a farm, the Adolfsons bought the Anoka County property. They hired a husband-wife team to tend the farm and soon amassed a dairy herd that was one of the top producers in Anoka County.

The Farmstead at Andover, Minnesota, sits on the site of the former Adolfson farm.

As the area grew, the Adolfsons began selling off their property for home construction, and by the early 1990s approximately ten acres remained of the original 360. Their son, David, by then a member of the Presbyterian Homes board, persuaded his family to sell the remaining acreage to PHS for construction of a retirement community. David's widowed mother immediately spoke for one of the cottages and lived out her days on her beloved farm. For Farmstead resident Ruth Le Noue, life on the Adolfson farm came full circle as well: Back in 1952, she and her husband, Vernon, were the couple that George Adolfson hired to live and work on the farm. As for the round barn, Presbyterian Homes leases it to an antiques shop owner. Preserved as a historic site, it is a constant reminder of Anoka County's proud pioneer legacy.

SUMMERHOUSE OF WOODBURY, 2000

Because the decision to build in Andover had been part of the Strategic Long Range Plan for some time, plans were put on hold in Woodbury, where SummerHouse, a seventy-seven-unit independent and congregate living community, had been in the works. A for-profit and a not-for-profit assisted living project had also recently opened in Woodbury, an eastern suburb of the Twin Cities, but research there had shown that a strong market for housing for older adults still existed in all categories, so the area remained a priority for additional development by Presbyterian Homes.

The $9.5 million SummerHouse of Woodbury opened in 2000, and is linked by skyway to Woodbury Central Park, which houses a YMCA, the Woodbury Community Center, and a Washington County Library. The indoor park features a waterfall, pond, and amphitheater. SummerHouse of Woodbury also contains a hair salon, a convenience store, and a media center, and offers recreational, social, and wellness programs. An assisted living addition is expected to open in the future, adding even more community space.

SUMMERHOUSE OF SHOREVIEW, 2000

In June 1999, a suspected arson at another SummerHouse—a seventy-two-unit independent living development in the St. Paul suburb of Shoreview—set back the occupancy timetable by six months. The $1.7 million fire at the complex, which Presbyterian Homes had been developing since 1997, was one of the costliest in Ramsey County history, and construction had to begin again almost from scratch. New occupants who were set to move in were temporarily housed in Oak Crest, Echo Ridge, and EagleCrest until SummerHouse of Shoreview could be rebuilt. Senior Housing Partners managed the development of the $8.2 million building, which sits on wooded land overlooking Lake Martha yet is near to stores, places of worship, and recreation spots.

CARDINAL POINTE MAPLEWOOD, 2000

Since 2000, Presbyterian Homes & Services has managed Cardinal Pointe, an independent living cooperative located in the St. Paul suburb of Maplewood. Owned by its residents, the building imparts a sense of southern hospitality, with its front porch

SummerHouse of Woodbury, Minnesota.

Cardinal Pointe of Maplewood, Minnesota.

SummerHouse of Shoreview, Minnesota.

and expansive grounds and flower gardens. Natural light floods the third-floor library through a distinctive cupola. The $12.7 million complex offers 108 moderate-cost apartments.

PRESBYTERIAN HOMES PARTNERS

In the autumn of 1997, Presbyterian Homes of Wisconsin and Presbyterian Homes of Minnesota began looking at ways for the two organizations to work together. There were two principal options. The organizations could become equal partners, with Minnesota concentrating on development and marketing (which was the Wisconsin group's preference), or the Minnesota organization could develop, own, and operate properties of its own in eastern Wisconsin, setting up a hub-and-spoke system. Market studies confirmed a significant opportunity, with demand for as many as 2,000 apartments for assisted living, congregate, and independent living over the next ten years. Milwaukee and its suburbs had several major for-profit providers, but most care was offered in stand-alone buildings, not continuum of care communities.

"We need to address the question of how . . . we can create a win-win for both organizations and to best meet the needs of services for older adults in the Milwaukee area," CEO Dan Lindh told the board, which proceeded in October 1999 with its commitment to help Presbyterian Homes of Wisconsin expand its presence in the Milwaukee area.

The new not-for-profit corporation—Presbyterian Homes Partners—developed a plan of operation. Each participant would have 50-percent equity in each project. Through Senior Housing Partners, Presbyterian Homes would market the projects, contribute its share of the equity, and provide management. And there would be an exit strategy: Presbyterian Homes of Wisconsin would buy out its partner over a period of time, but the Minnesota organization would have first right of refusal, guaranteeing it full ownership if desired.

Thus, as the twenty-first century dawned, Presbyterian Homes was poised for a new era of growth. Presbyterian Homes of Wisconsin had become a partner with its Minnesota counterpart in seeking development opportunities in and around Milwaukee. Further developments were under way in the western and southern hubs of the Twin Cities metropolitan area. A long-envisioned eastern hub was about to fully emerge, with projects in Little Canada, Woodbury, and Oakdale already providing an initial presence. On the horizon was Boutwells Landing, a 590-unit continuum of care hub community in the St. Croix Valley that was a partnership between Presbyterian Homes, Lakeview Hospital, and Croixdale Residence. Its consequences were profound, inspiring other continuum of care developments within the organization and solidifying Presbyterian Homes' national reputation as a premier provider of elder care.

Through partnerships with various hospitals, churches, and communities, Presbyterian Homes was strengthening its full continuum of care campuses in Minnesota and beyond. At the same time, it was breaking ground at last for the expanded care center in Bloomington, thus completing the Gideon Pond Center campus it had helped begin thirty years earlier.

The time had arrived for PHS to harvest the fruit of its faithful labors.

CHAPTER FIVE

A Time to Reap

PARTNERING AND MANAGING

Kirkland Crossings in Pewaukee, Wisconsin.

WHEN THE SYNOD OF Lakes and Prairies approved the name "Presbyterian Homes & Services" on January 19, 1999, it recognized the broader scope of the organization's mission. Through Presbyterian Homes Partners, an affiliation with Presbyterian Homes of Wisconsin, PHS was developing properties to manage in the Milwaukee area. Through partnerships with hospitals, churches, and communities, PHS was strengthening its full continuum of care campuses in Minnesota, Iowa, and western Wisconsin. One such campus in the Twin Cities—the Bloomington Care Center—would at last break ground, thus completing the Gideon Pond Center community envisioned thirty years earlier.

THE DEERFIELD NEW RICHMOND, WISCONSIN, 1999

The purchase of Mill Pond in Ankeny, Iowa, was followed two years later by another out-of-state transaction, this one in the western Wisconsin community of New Richmond. In 1999, Presbyterian Homes & Services agreed to be a fifty-fifty partner with Holy Family Hospital to develop and manage The Deerfield, which consists of fifty independent living apartments and thirty-two assisted living apartments in a countrylike setting on five acres. When The Deerfield opened in September of that year, it was viewed as a community with long-term growth potential and strategic importance.

RESIDENT PROFILE

Carl and Fay Nordin

When retired postmaster Carl Nordin of Siren, Wisconsin, spent six weeks in a skilled care center recuperating from a broken ankle, he and his wife, Fay, knew they would need to move out of their house and into a handicapped-accessible apartment. In 2003, they moved into The Deerfield in nearby New Richmond. "My husband liked it from day one," Fay recalls. Just two years later, Carl passed away. In her living room she keeps the folded American flag that graced his coffin, a proud reminder of his service to his country during World War II.

Carl was on furlough to marry Fay when his leave was suddenly cancelled. He was shipped to the Philippines, where he was captured by the Japanese after their attack on Pearl Harbor. A POW for two years, he labored in parasite-ridden rice fields and a freezing smelter. As a result, and despite the kindnesses of a Japanese guard, Carl suffered poor health for nearly the rest of his life.

The Deerfield in New Richmond, Wisconsin.

Deerfield Commons is part of the larger New Richmond campus.

When at last he was to sail home, he saw his compassionate captor at the dock, waving and crying. Twenty-five years later, the same guard greeted Carl and Fay at the old POW camps during a reunion for peace.

When he was eighty years old, Carl wrote *We Were Next to Nothing,* a memoir based on the diary he kept as a prisoner of war. He shared his story with high school students as well as several other WWII veterans living at The Deerfield.

Avalon Square in Waukesha, Wisconsin.

KIRKLAND CROSSINGS PEWAUKEE, WISCONSIN, 2001

In 1999, after Presbyterian Homes and Presbyterian Homes of Wisconsin formed their affiliation known as Presbyterian Homes Partners, they focused on developing properties in the Milwaukee area. By December 1999, PHS agreed to take on the marketing, development, and construction of Kirkland Crossings, a twelve-acre, 142-unit community of townhomes and independent living apartments and assisted living apartments in Pewaukee, about twenty miles west of downtown Milwaukee.

"We have identified it as an outstanding opportunity and starting point," CEO Dan Lindh told the board. "By partnering on the first project, we can set a tone for future working relationships, see how the synergy might unfold, and give the Presbyterian Homes of Wisconsin board confidence as they begin their first project in the last twenty-five years."

PHS would also manage Kirkland Crossings, and provide consulting services across a wide spectrum, including fund-raising, human relations, quality control, a leadership institute, and general support. Kirkland Crossings opened officially in May 2001, although part of the community was completed the previous fall. The $17.1 million campus consists of twenty-two townhomes,

Corner apartments at Avalon Square.

Avalon Square's exercise room.

sixty independent living apartments, and sixty assisted living apartments, including twenty for memory care.

AVALON SQUARE WAUKESHA, 2003

Completed in April 2003, Avalon Square sits on the former site of two historic hotels: the 1871 National (renamed the Waukesha Hotel) and the 1927 Avalon Manor. Located in Waukesha, Wisconsin, about fifteen miles west of downtown Milwaukee, the Avalon Manor was a one-time luxury hotel that was acquired by Presbyterian Homes of Wisconsin

A 1950s-style cafe in Avalon Square.

Avalon Square chapel.

Avalon Square's courtyard.

in 1968 as a housing complex for older adults. A twenty-two-bed skilled care center was added to the property in 1970.

Thirty-three years later, with assistance from Presbyterian Homes & Services on development, marketing, and management, Avalon Manor became part of Avalon Square. The campus now anchors Waukesha's central business area, giving older adults the opportunity to live within walking distance of restaurants, retail shops and services, parks, cultural activities, churches, and a beautiful river walk. The downtown location offers a new standard for senior residential living.

The design of the 147-unit complex celebrates the heritage of both hotels. Architects carefully preserved the Waukesha Hotel's original three-story exterior design, for instance, including a decorative cupola. The limestone exterior was dismantled stone by stone and reassembled on the new building, which also incorporated the Waukesha Hotel's original foundation. The hotel's historic neon sign was reinstalled in the new 2,500-square-foot fitness center.

The interior of Avalon Square blends state-of-the-art amenities with reminders of times past. A lounge resembles an English sitting room that existed in one of the old hotels, and a café-deli represents a 1950s-era coffee shop. As part of the downtown arts scene, a permanent gallery in the lobby showcases a changing exhibit of artistic achievements of residents and local artists as well as artifacts from Waukesha's history. The 28,000-square-foot town center quickly became a downtown destination for residents and other older adults in the community as a place to enjoy organized physical, social, and intellectual activities and services.

Once the $24.2 million Avalon Square was completed, Avalon Manor was renovated to include memory care and community-based residential care. The continuum of care campus now consists of sixty-eight apartments for independent living, fifty-two for residential care, and twenty-seven for specialty care; it also includes an on-site adult daycare center. In 2003, the American Institute of Architects' Design for Aging Center presented Avalon Square with its Citation of Merit Award. The campus was awarded the citation for creating a sense of community in a dwelling that blends commercial space, historic preservation, and urban living.

ST. ANDREW'S VILLAGE MAHTOMEDI, 2001

In the late 1990s parishioners of St. Andrew's Evangelical Lutheran Church, a congregation of 9,500 in the St. Paul suburb of Mahtomedi, asked themselves what they should be doing for their elderly members. As aging church members moved to retirement complexes in Minneapolis and St. Paul, not only was a valuable membership base gone, but it also became increasingly difficult for pastoral staff to minister to those who had moved away. The older congregants themselves wanted to stay in the Mahtomedi community and continue participating in the life of their church. The church's solution was to build a retirement home on fourteen acres of land that adjoined its property.

St. Andrew's turned to Presbyterian Homes to form a partnership, which was launched in 1999 following a market study that determined a strong need for assisted living and senior housing services in Mahtomedi and the neighboring suburb of White Bear Lake.

St. Andrew's Village.

St. Andrew's Village in Mahtomedi, Minnesota.

Residents Walter and Joan Hanson at Boutwells Landing in Oak Park Heights, Minnesota.

Boutwells Landing square.

Discussions with the city of Mahtomedi further indicated that tax-exempt funding would be available. Presbyterian Homes' interest in proceeding with the project was also high because of the area's proximity to PHS's Woodbury development and its overall strategy for expanding services in Washington County and the St. Croix Valley.

The partnership proceeded, with Presbyterian Homes & Services as part owner as well as developer, marketer, and manager of the $16.7 million Mahtomedi community, now called St. Andrew's Village. The seventy independent living apartments opened in January 2001; the forty-four assisted living apartments and town center opened in February 2002. The Arbor, a memory care center for twenty-five, soon followed, as did a child development center. A pastor from St. Andrew's Church serves as chaplain at the community, where he conducts Sunday services (including special services for memory care residents) and weekly Bible study classes.

BOUTWELLS LANDING OAK PARK HEIGHTS, 2002

In the summer of 1997, Presbyterian Homes began intensive preparations for developing the fourth hub-and-spoke system in its Twin Cities market. The organization was now well established in the north, south, and west. Development of Echo Ridge was under way, and management of The Deerfield would soon be a reality. Washington County and the St. Croix Valley were the next areas of focus.

Research had shown that demand for services for older adults would increase as much as 353 percent in the St. Croix Valley over the next two decades. It also indicated that the Valley lacked a broad range of services for older adults, and that the few services that did exist—such as the Croixdale Residence—could be better integrated. Established in 1956 as the Washington County Association for Senior Citizens, Croixdale was the Upper Midwest's first "board and care" retirement community. The complex was started by Katherine B. Andersen, Betty Hulings, and other concerned citizens of the St. Croix Valley to offer affordable retirement housing to residents of the area.

It appeared that if a group of providers were to form a service organization with Presbyterian Homes, its hub-and-spoke concept could be applied to the broader geographic area of Washington County and the St. Croix Valley. The resulting continuum of care community would be far more extensive than any one provider could supply. Presbyterian Homes and Croixdale thus joined with Lakeview Hospital of Stillwater in 1997, forming a nonprofit organization called Valley Senior Services Alliance to

Benefactor Katherine B. Andersen.

Wetlands and a nature preserve are part of the grounds at Boutwells Landing.

Boutwells Landing garden.

build the community. Presbyterian Homes would own 70 percent of the new campus. Lakeview Hospital would own 20 percent and be the provider of home care, pharmacy, and other care-related services. Croixdale would own 10 percent and bring its experience and knowledge of the region to the equation. In addition to the three owners, other providers included Warm World Childcare and Circle of Friends adult daycare, Meals on Wheels, Courage Center, Washington County Historical Society, and Stillwater Adult Community Education.

PARTNER PROFILE

Lakeview Hospital

When in 1984 the Minnesota Legislature issued a moratorium on adding nursing home beds in the state, Lakeview Hospital CEO Kurt Giesler foresaw that assisted living housing would become the "nursing home of the future." "We wanted to get into that business, but we didn't know anything about senior housing," Giesler says. Seeking help in 1997 in developing such housing, he met with Presbyterian Homes, which proposed a far more comprehensive vision: a full continuum of care campus in Oak Park Heights that would include independent living and long-term care as well as assisted living. Lakeview partnered with Presbyterian Homes and Bayport-based Croixdale in the development of the campus, known as Boutwells Landing.

"Our partnership with Presbyterian Homes has exceeded our expectations," Giesler says. The Stillwater hospital provides many services at Boutwells Landing, including hospice, home care, diabetes education, and cardiac rehabilitation programs. "We just opened a hospice care service we call 'The Gathering,'" he says, adding that Lakeview may also establish a physicians' clinic at Boutwells. "It has been a great time—positive, fun—and a wonderful service to the community. I would live there in a heartbeat."

In December 1997 the Presbyterian Homes board authorized the purchase of land to begin the first phase of the project, named Boutwells Landing after William Thurston Boutwell. This pastor of Stillwater's First Presbyterian Church had been a significant contributor to the life and welfare of the residents in the St. Croix Valley area in the mid-1800s.

HISTORY PROFILE
William Thurston Boutwell

After he was ordained a Congregationalist minister in 1831, William Thurston Boutwell—a twenty-eight-year-old New Hampshire native—headed west to work among the Chippewa Indians of Michigan, Wisconsin, and Minnesota. While the missionary was stationed on Michigan's Upper Peninsula, scientist-explorer Henry Rowe Schoolcraft asked him to accompany his party in locating the source of the Mississippi River. When they found it at Elk Lake in northern Minnesota, Schoolcraft asked Boutwell to give him the Latin words for "true" *(veritas)* and "head" *(caput)*. Joining and contracting the two words, Schoolcraft renamed the river's headwaters Lake Itasca.

Congregationalists and Presbyterians often cooperated in mission work, as was the case with Boutwell and Schoolcraft. On his way down the Mississippi, Boutwell stopped at Fort Snelling, where he met the boat on which Gideon Hollister Pond and his brother, Samuel, were arriving to begin their work among the Dakota Indians. The three soon became close friends.

Reverend Boutwell traveled on to Lake Pokegama, near Pine City, Minnesota, where he and his wife, Hester, joined missionaries already stationed there. When it became increasingly difficult for them to establish schools and churches, the mission station was abandoned. The Boutwells bought a farm near Stillwater, Minnesota, in hopes of supporting their nine children. There, in 1849, Reverend Boutwell helped establish the First Presbyterian Church. He died in 1890, having been a faithful servant of Stillwater's citizens for more than fifty years.

Reverend William Thurston Boutwell.

By April 1998, land in Oak Park Heights was under option for purchase, an architect was hired, and the project's four phases of

Swanson Memorial Chapel at Boutwells Landing.

construction were refined. The plan called for establishing a hub of services in the Stillwater area, with spokes covering other regions, specifically Washington County, but also communities in western Wisconsin. The hub would consist first of congregate housing, including assisted living and memory care at Boutwells Landing. The second phase would include townhomes, a medical clinic, aquatic therapy, subacute care, low-income assisted living apartments in Washington County, and adult daycare at Boutwells Landing and other sites in the area. It would be the largest project undertaken in the history of Presbyterian Homes. At $94.6 million, it would also be the costliest.

By October 1998, several foundations had pledged $4.35 million for the project, followed by $46 million in bond issues by the city of Oak Park Heights, a guarantee of $2.8 million from Valley Senior Services Alliance, and a guarantee of $40 million from Presbyterian Homes. By December 1999, fifty-six townhomes were completed; by the fall of 2001 The Commons, a sixty-five-unit assisted living building, and twenty-nine memory care apartments had opened; and The Terrace, a 101-unit independent living complex, opened in February 2002. The town center opened in summer 2003 and includes a bank, a retail establishment modeled on the Country Store, a branch of the Stillwater Public Library, an auditorium and a community learning center, and exhibits arranged by the Washington County Historical Society. Community-related services such as adult and child daycare, Meals on Wheels, and health care and hospice services are also available.

The town center at Boutwells Landing also houses the Swanson Memorial Chapel, a gift from the Swanson family in memory of Earl Swanson, former CEO of the Andersen Corporation. The chapel features five stained-glass windows designed by Michael Pilla of St. Paul's Monarch Studios and was built by Cardinal Glass of Amery, Wisconsin, a firm long associated with Andersen Windows. Feauring tall white pines set against a deep blue sky, the windows encircle the nave, suggesting the serenity of a grove. The simple wood furnishings were custom-crafted by McLaughlin Woodworking of Maple Plain, Minnesota. The organ, which once graced the Swanson home, was donated by Nyda Swanson, Earl's wife and now a resident of Boutwells Landing. Chaplains and ministers from area churches offer several ecumenical services every week in the chapel.

Construction of McKean Square at Boutwells Landing—eighty-one village and coach homes and seventy-eight brownstone flats—was completed in the spring of 2005. Its walking trails and extensively landscaped grounds are part of the larger Boutwells community, situated on 118 acres of farmland that Woodbury native Elmer Haase bought in 1942. After his death in 1997, Haase's family sold some of that land to Presbyterian Homes; the heart of that acreage was later named the Haase Nature Preserve. Now a part of the Oak Park Heights Parks and Trails system, the prairie land includes many mature oaks and evergreens adjacent to wetlands. Deer, hawks, and other wildlife are common sights. Ponds, birdhouses, and benches in the preserve and behind the central Boutwells Landing building add to the pleasantness of the surroundings. A reconstruction of Reverend William Thurston Boutwell's 1849 First Presbyterian Church of Stillwater and of the old McKean schoolhouse will be built at Boutwells Landing in the village square in the near future.

FAMILY PROFILE
Marge Ashbach

It's not uncommon for more than one branch of a family to live at PHS. For siblings Marge Ashbach and Carl Duberg, that tradition started back when their sister, Helen, became a resident at Presbyterian Homes of Arden Hills. Marge moved into Boutwells Landing in 2002 following the death of her husband, Robert, a Minnesota state senator and Presbyterian Homes board member. After visiting his sister Marge at her new home, Carl and his wife, Beatrice, decided to leave their home in 2004 for Boutwells Landing. "We liked what we saw and decided to move in," Carl says.

Resident Marge Ashbach with bridegroom Robert.

Entrance to Presbyterian Homes of Inver Grove Heights.

Presbyterian Homes of Inver Grove Heights, Minnesota.

Marge admits she was amazed at the swift decision of her typically more circumspect brother, a retired naval captain who had moved out east in 1942 to enroll at the U.S. Naval Academy. "They came out here from Virginia to visit, looked over the place, and moved in—just like that," she says. Brother and sister now live just minutes apart: Carl in one of the brownstones with Beatrice, and Marge in an assisted living apartment.

PRESBYTERIAN HOMES OF INVER GROVE HEIGHTS, 2002

As Presbyterian Homes was in the midst of developing Boutwells Landing, the mayor of Inver Grove Heights extended an invitation to PHS to develop a $38.1 million continuum of care community in his city. The twenty-seven-acre site was to include townhomes as well as apartments for independent living, assisted living, and memory care. The concept was in line with PHS's strategic plan and virtually identical to the mini-continuum of care development the organization had earlier planned for Dakota County.

By October 2002, the Terrace—ninety independent living apartments—was completed, followed in February 2003 by The Commons, a building with eighty-six assisted living apartments. The Arbor memory care apartments opened a few months later; diabetes care was soon added. Living spaces are linked via The Lodge town center, whose BlueBeary Café, Bear Necessities General Store, and Wildwood Chapel impart that cabin-in-the-north-woods feel. Exposed log beams and cultured field stone are used throughout the complex, which stands on the former site of the historic Krech-Korfhage Farm.

Interviewed shortly before the campus opened, Gladys Krech Byrnes—a descendant of the original owner—fondly recalled growing up on the farmland's beautiful expanse of natural wetlands and woods. Byrnes's great-great-grandparents, Johannes and Barbara Krech, emigrated from Germany to America in 1852 and settled briefly in New Jersey before moving to the Territory of Minnesota two years later. There, they filed claim on forty acres in Inver Grove Heights. In time, seven generations of the family took up residence on nearby farms. Byrnes was born on the original farm in 1920. Her father, Louis Jr., inherited the farm in 1924 and lived and worked there until the 1930s, when he lost the property during the Great Depression. The farm was purchased by Robert and Lois Korfhage and eventually sold to Presbyterian Homes & Services.

HIGHLAND RIDGE WILLIAMSBURG, IOWA, 2004

As the Oak Park Heights and Inver Grove Heights campuses were under construction, Presbyterian Homes & Services was approached in October 2001 by the Roland and Ruby Holden Family Foundation about assisting with the development of a continuum of care campus in the community of Williamsburg, Iowa, twenty miles west of Iowa City. The foundation envisioned a development similar in size to The Deerfield and comparable in amenities and construction to Boutwells Landing. The Holden Foundation had a long-standing history of

Highland Ridge in Williamsburg, Iowa.

Ruby Holden (left) and son Ron Holden (center) at the Highland Ridge ribbon-cutting ceremony.

philanthropy, making generous donations to the Holden Comprehensive Cancer Center and the Roland and Ruby Holden Cancer Research Laboratories at the University of Iowa, as well as to local school projects, athletic facilities, and scholarships. Now, the Holden Foundation was prepared to make a $10 million grant and help finance Highland Ridge, as the complex was to be called.

Marketing surveys in Cedar Rapids, Iowa City, the Amana Colonies, and other communities within a thirty-mile radius of Williamsburg suggested that a significant opportunity existed to develop a hub-and-spoke system in southeastern Iowa. Presbyterian Homes now owns and manages the $19.5 million development.

Highland Ridge opened in January 2004. The 170-acre site includes fifty apartments for independent living and thirty-six apartments for assisted living, as well as several memory care and respite care suites. A village square houses beauty and barber shops, a café, and a grocery, all named after businesses and people in Williamsburg. The campus also includes a chapel, gardens, and a child daycare center where residents regularly stop by to rock the babies. Expansion plans include a skilled care center and townhomes.

DONOR PROFILE

Roland and Ruby Holden

Roland and Ruby Holden had envisioned building a retirement community in Williamsburg, Iowa, so that family and friends in their small town would not be separated when age or illness forced them from their homes. The Holdens' dreams began to come true in 2002, when ground was broken for Highland Ridge.

The saga began with farmers Carl and Augusta Holden, whose son Carl and grandson Roland launched Holden's Foundation Seeds, which became a major employer in Williamsburg. Roland's son Ron took over management of the four-generation company until it was sold in 1997 to Monsanto. Soon Ron and his wife, Arlene, began to fulfill his parents' vision. After purchasing 170 acres, they asked Presbyterian Homes to help them develop Highland Ridge. The family designed everything, Arlene says, from choosing pastel wall colors to positioning large windows to overlook reflecting pools. Although Roland did not live to see the building completed, Ruby Holden—now a resident of the home—cut the ribbon at the dedication.

True to their word, the Holden family made Highland Ridge a dream come true for many of Williamsburg's retired residents: they established an endowment fund to ensure that, in Arlene's words, "anyone can live here."

CROIXDALE BAYPORT, 2004

In 1983, Croixdale had asked Presbyterian Homes for help in building an apartment complex. In April 2003, Croixdale again invited PHS to share its expertise, this time to remodel the same building into fifty-six independent living apartments. As planning progressed, however, it was determined that building a new complex would produce better results. Residents were relocated while an assisted living building was constructed; work on a new independent living building followed. Residents returned to new surroundings in the fall of 2004 and the spring of 2005. During this time the Croixdale board determined that the future for residents would best be served by formalizing a direct affiliation with Presbyterian Homes & Services.

The Holden family. Seated, from left: Arlene Holden, Ron Holden, Susan Holden-McCurry, Ruby Holden, Kathy Holden, Karol Holden. Back row: Austin Blythe, Corbin Blythe, Mary Holden-Blythe, Curt Blythe, Joe McCurry, Sveta McCurry, Dave McCurry, Holden Blythe, Trenton Blythe.

SUMMERWOOD OF CHANHASSEN, 2004

Planning began in earnest in 2001 for SummerWood of Chanhassen, a $27.9 million continuum of care development adjacent to St. Hubert Catholic Church in the Twin Cities suburb of Chanhassen. With Catholic Eldercare, the church had joined Presbyterian Homes & Services in a partnership to serve elders in the St. Hubert congregation. Ninety independent living apartments at SummerWood of Chanhassen opened in October 2004; seventy-one assisted living apartments, including eighteen for memory care, opened in February 2005.

SummerWood of Chanhassen, Minnesota.

The campus includes a café, theater, fitness center, and beauty salon. Rented retail space is part of the larger surrounding village center. Chanhassen Catholic Housing, a 20-percent partner, has the option to buy the property in 2013, while Presbyterian Homes & Services holds the remaining 80 percent.

SUMMERWOOD OF PLYMOUTH, 2004

The Department of Housing and Urban Development and the Wedum Foundation again turned to Presbyterian Homes & Services in the summer of 2004, asking the organization to acquire The Regent at Plymouth, located in the Minneapolis suburb of Plymouth. While some residents had moved into The Regent's independent living and assisted living apartments, the memory care program at the 120-unit mini-continuum of care community had not opened; it was in technical default with HUD and had incurred too much debt. By that fall, PHS purchased the $18.7 million

SummerWood of Plymouth, Minnesota.

development and renamed it SummerWood of Plymouth. By January 2005, all apartments—sixty-eight for independent living, twenty-eight for assisted living, twenty-four for memory care—were operational.

SummerWood of Plymouth became a striking example of the flexibility and speed with which the board of Presbyterian Homes & Services could conduct business if it deemed that the circumstances and the opportunity were right.

PRESBYTERIAN HOMES OF BLOOMINGTON, 2005

In December 2000, Presbyterian Homes moved toward the long-awaited replacement of the Bloomington Care Center, but the scope of the Phase IV component of the original Gideon Pond Center campus—including key elements of the care center and the nature and extent of community services—needed clarification. The decision to rebuild the eighty-bed residential care center came just four years after Presbyterian

Homes had acquired the thirty-year-old Eagle Nursing Home, which it had planned to replace. That decision required PHS to confront state-imposed construction restrictions that for twenty years had sought to end overbuilding in the industry through a moratorium on nursing-home construction. By April 2001, Presbyterian Homes had secured Moratorium Exception Process Approval funding and tax-exempt financing. This lifted the construction restriction and allowed replacement of existing beds and the new care center at Presbyterian Homes of Bloomington to be built.

There was significant support for this initiative, which moved successfully through several rounds of committee hearings. The

The long-awaited care center at Presbyterian Homes of Bloomington, Minnesota, completes the campus's continuum of care community.

advocates were the Minnesota Department of Health and the city of Bloomington and its Housing Rehabilitation Authority. The moratorium exception was approved. Opened in September 2005, the $28.3 million, ninety-eight-unit care center is a model for older adult care, differing dramatically from other PHS projects. Each private apartment has its own bathroom and kitchenette; "household" groups of ten apartments provide for socializing, meals, and other gatherings. An assisted living wing provides memory care for eighteen. The complex includes a town center with a three-level rotunda, a wellness and fitness center, and a pool. Also included are a chapel, general store, museum, library, bank, theater, game room, and other amenities. The care center and memory care wing are linked to the Gideon Pond independent living apartments, the Gardens assisted living apartments, and the Newton Manor apartments for independent and assisted living.

Envisioned thirty years ago, the dream of a full continuum of care Bloomington campus has been fully realized. Indeed, the seed that was Presbyterian Homes in 1955 has matured and flourished.

DONOR PROFILE

John and Dolores Holl

As president of Seeger Refrigeration, John Holl orchestrated the 1955 sale of his successful St. Paul business to the Whirlpool Company. Through the years, he and his wife, Dolores, kept a modest philanthropic profile. But a 1999 newspaper account of the estate the Holls left to several charities identified it as a "stunning legacy"—one of the biggest charitable gifts in recent Minnesota history.

Part of the Holl estate—$29 million—was given to Presbyterian Homes & Services; the couple had no children. As residents of Presbyterian Homes of Arden Hills for seven years, the couple knew firsthand the mission of PHS. Their gift has supported the Chaplaincy Endowment, Quality of Life Initiatives, the Mission Benevolence Fund, and capital improvements at various campuses, as well as new developments such as The Arbor at EagleCrest, Boutwells Landing, and the innovative care center at Presbyterian Homes of Bloomington.

An Eye to the Future

FOR ITS FIRST THIRTY YEARS of existence, Presbyterian Homes & Services had but one elder care community, "way out in the country" in the St. Paul suburb of Arden Hills. In its thirtieth year, Presbyterian Homes opened a community in Bloomington, in the Twin Cities southern metropolitan area. In the two decades that followed, the organization bought or developed more than thirty more sites in Minnesota, Iowa, and Wisconsin. Now, in its fiftieth year of service to older adults, Presbyterian Homes & Services continues to maintain its steadfast purpose and its commitment to quality and innovation. It has become a regional model with aspirations to become a world-class innovator in housing, health care, and training.

FUTURE TWIN CITIES PROJECTS

Several Presbyterian Homes projects are in various stages of progress throughout the Twin Cities metropolitan area:

Presbyterian Homes of North Oaks, a 172-unit continuum-of-care retirement community similar to Boutwells Landing, is scheduled to open in late 2005. With its Old English feel, the design of the complex has already won accolades from *The Business Journal,* which declared Presbyterian Homes of North Oaks its 2004 winner in the Multifamily Residential Development category.

The property is built on five tracts of land on twenty-two acres in North Oaks, a suburb north of St. Paul. The first tract contains eighty-four apartments for independent living, forty-four for assisted living, and fourteen for memory care, as well as a child care center; its town center features a market, a sidewalk café, a conservatory, a fitness center and pool, a learning center and auditorium, a theater, and a chapel. The second tract contains nine buildings of eight condominiums each, patterned after the Mews of London. The third tract houses offices of the North Oaks Company, a restaurant called Tria, a wellness center where skilled care therapies (physical, speech, occupational) will be available, and twenty-two skilled care suites. The North Oaks Company has donated the fourth tract to the North Oaks Home Owners Association for a soccer field, community gardens, a band shell, and a pavilion. The fifth tract constitutes the major roadways. The total investment in the North Oaks campus is just over $85 million—the second most expensive project undertaken to date by Presbyterian Homes & Services.

Located near the shores of Wilkinson Lake, Presbyterian Homes of North Oaks sits on land once owned by James J. Hill. In 1883, Hill—owner of the Great Northern Railroad, investor in Minnesota's Iron Range—purchased the 3,500-acre North Oaks site from the city of St. Paul, which had bought it the previous year from pioneer C. D. Gilfillan. Gilfillan had intended to preserve a land, wildlife, and water area that provided fresh water to St. Paul, and Hill honored that goal. At the same time, Hill established a model experimental farm in North Oaks, where he developed superior livestock and devised methods to help settlers who lived near his

The Hill family farm in North Oaks, Minnesota.

James J. Hill.

railroads improve their crop yields. Hill's son Louis succeeded him at the farm, maintaining its emphasis on conservation. In 1950, Louis's children, led by Louis Jr., formed the North Oaks Company. Its continuing aim is to maintain a wildlife habitat and to promote a unique system of conservation, engineering, and residential planning. The city of North Oaks, incorporated in 1956, was designated as a game refuge; a select herd of red deer is farmed within the city's agricultural area. In 1999 the North Oaks Company dedicated 885 acres of permanent open space to the city and to the North Oaks Home Owners Association, of which 620 acres remain a natural conservation area. Presbyterian Homes of North Oaks has taken a principled approach to the preservation of nature on the campus.

The architecture of Presbyterian Homes of North Oaks has an Old English look and feel.

North Oaks groundbreaking. Front row from left: resident Joan Krogh; Carolyn McCann, North Oaks Company; Jeff Peterson, US Bank; resident Dorothy Dokmo; Gary Eagles, North Oaks Company; Bill Campbell, North Oaks Planning Commission; Dick Hara, North Oaks Home Owners Association; Dan Lindh, Presbyterian Homes. Back row: resident Les Krogh; Bill Chadwick, Presbyterian Homes; Dave Adolfson, Adolfson & Peterson; Mike Bingham, Presbyterian Homes board; Brook Adolfson; Tim Dunleavy, North Oaks City Council; Jim March, City of North Oaks; Mark Petit, North Oaks Home Owners Association; Kirk Velett, In-Site Architect; Brad Wert, Piper Jaffray; North Oaks mayor Thomas Watson.

SummerWood of Cottage Grove is scheduled to open in 2007. The St. Paul suburb of Cottage Grove endorsed Presbyterian Homes in 2003 to redevelop Cottage Square Mall in the city's original commercial area. Cottage Grove approved full tax increment financing, commitments of $1.9 million from the Andersen Foundation and other sources were in place by mid-2004, and the purchase was completed that November. A 140-unit complex is envisioned, with up to ninety

The North Oaks residence dining area.

North Oaks garden.

apartments for independent living, forty-two for assisted living, and eighteen for memory care, as well as a 40,000-square-foot retail area.

SummerHouse of Roseville, located in the Hamline Center, is expected to begin construction in the spring of 2007. Up to ninety-five independent living apartments, plus 13,500 feet of commercial and retail space, will be built in the strip mall space adjacent to PHS's administrative offices.

Shepherd's Path, a major retirement campus in Scott County, Minnesota, is under discussion at this time. The project would be a partnership between PHS and Shepherd of the Lake Lutheran Church in Prior Lake.

Westminster Presbyterian Church in Minneapolis continues its conversations with PHS regarding construction of a nearby high-rise building that will offer a full continuum of housing and services, including independent living, assisted living, and a care center.

NATIONAL PROSPECTS

Presbyterian Homes' decision to work with the Holden Foundation on Highland Ridge in Williamsburg, Iowa, and PHS's involvement in the metropolitan area of Milwaukee, Wisconsin, were strong signs of the organization's increasing confidence in responding to challenges that lay well outside its primary market area. Each new project had to make economic sense in the relatively short run; if it did not, the mission and spiritual foundation of PHS itself could eventually be compromised.

Through its development arm—Senior Housing Partners—Presbyterian Homes has been called on to assist other faith-based providers in various locations. PHS has been involved in projects in New Jersey; Grand Forks, North Dakota, following the 1997 flood; Seattle, Washington; Council Bluffs, Iowa; Duluth and Rochester, Minnesota; and other areas.

LOOKING AHEAD

With the completion of projects in progress—particularly in Bloomington, North Oaks, and Oak Park Heights, Minnesota—the number of people served by Presbyterian Homes & Services will likely increase by 25 percent, to approximately 10,000 individuals, by 2012. In the wake of its growth during the previous decade, PHS needed to decide whether to continue to expand beyond the Twin Cities metropolitan area and out of state, whether partnerships would remain a good idea, and whether specific elements of the Strategic Long Range Plan, implemented in 1991 and regularly revised, should again be updated.

One in eight Minnesotans was sixty-five or older in 1990. By 2030, one in four Minnesotans—1.2 million persons—will be over sixty-five, with baby boomers sparking growth greatly in this age category beginning in 2010, particularly in the Twin Cities area. The market for housing for older Minnesotans at the start of the twenty-first century is therefore strong, particularly for cooperative condominiums and townhomes geared toward active and independent older adults. The market for moderately priced housing for older Minnesotans will be substantial, especially in the inner city. First- and second-ring suburbs continue to require all types of services for older adults. While service-intensive housing will not see the same growth, the need will continue at a steady level, especially in continuum of care settings where residents living independently gradually require more services. Between 2020 and 2030, the number of Minnesotans over the age of eighty-five will increase by 34 percent. Between 2030 and 2040 it will increase another 58 percent, to 163,000 individuals, and by 2050 it will be 250,000.

Keeping in mind the significant increase in the older population, Presbyterian Homes concluded that it needed to continue developing housing for older adults, with campuses offering integrated services as the primary focus. It also should become more involved with urban and mixed-use construction that provides affordable housing for lower-income older adults, use partnerships to achieve market share in locations consistent with its strategic plan, and complete its hub-and-spoke sites in Minnesota, Wisconsin, and Iowa. This means establishing 2,000 more assisted living apartments in Milwaukee and 1,000 throughout Iowa, as well as developing market-rate and low-income projects in downtown Minneapolis. General geographic expansion, PHS decided, is appropriate. With increased needs, redevelopment of the older buildings in Arden Hills and Minnetonka, Minnesota, and Ankeny, Iowa, is essential.

A LEADER IN LEGISLATIVE REFORM

The role of Presbyterian Homes & Services as a regional and national leader in seeking reform of long-term care policy has grown over the years, particularly since the late 1990s. Senior PHS management, led by CEO Dan Lindh, has participated in discussions with state and national leaders in health care, housing, and government to push reform of state and federal regulations that govern skilled care as well as Medicare and Medicaid reimbursement. The current systems are complex, expensive, and outdated, having been designed to provide care primarily via traditional skilled care centers, which no longer meet the needs of residents or providers. A transformation of services for older adults—to make them more consumer-driven and community-oriented—is necessary for the future.

In addition, as chair of the Minnesota Health and Housing Alliance for 2004–2005, Lindh has provided statewide and national leadership in transforming the structure of financing and services for older adults. MHHA is a statewide trade association of providers of a complete continuum of services for older adults, including long-term care, senior housing with supportive services, and community-based services.

Board chair Sally Howard.

Current board chair Sally Howard regards Presbyterian Homes & Services as consistently having been the right organization in the right place at the right time. For fifty years, and particularly since major expansion began in the 1980s, PHS has not simply *provided* care for the elderly, Howard says. It has, in the most profound sense, *understood* care for the elderly. More than anything else, she says, this has meant recognizing how elder care can be less institutional in its emphasis, and, consequently, a better experience. In Howard's view, "genius ideas" have emerged from among the staff, and these ideas have been successfully implemented within a demanding financial context that requires the organization to do as much as possible with whatever funds are available.

THE PROVIDER AND EMPLOYER OF CHOICE

Fifty years after Presbyterian Homes was founded, it continues to be perceived as a leader in the community. Other faith-based, not-for-profit providers throughout the nation routinely ask the PHS management staff to help identify and define the ever-changing needs of older adults, and to partner in developing housing and services to meet those needs.

In the face of future growth, says CEO Dan Lindh, Presbyterian Homes & Services not only aspires to be the provider of choice, but also a model of education and training for other organizations. In training its employees, PHS management has four broad goals: to be the provider of choice, to be the employer of choice, to have efficient and effective services, and to nurture a Christian culture. Two strategies used to reach those goals are the practice of Stand Up and classes through the Leadership Institute.

Stand Up consists of an informal daily meeting, no longer than ten to fifteen minutes, that reinforces the mission statement of Presbyterian Homes & Services:

"The services provided will be of the highest quality and designed to promote independence, dignity, and well-being. The emphasis will be on innovation and leadership in providing compassionate and highly competent care with the inspiration of God's love and word."

As employees gather in a hallway or office, supervisors or staff follow a script that may include news of the organization or the site, congratulations to staff with birthdays and employment anniversaries, and an anecdote reinforcing the ideals contained in the PHS mission statement. It may be a note of thanks from a family of a resident, a reminder of a donor's generosity, or an example of an employee's hard work. The strategy was adapted from the Ritz-Carlton Hotel Company, a winner of the Malcolm Baldrige National Quality Award, established by Congress in 1987 to honor Ronald Reagan's secretary of commerce.

Each new employee is given a pocket-sized card with the PHS motto *("Creating smiles in the eyes of our residents")* and the organization's statement of purpose *("To give personalized attention to the well-being of each resident, while enhancing their independence and dignity").* It also contains three promises the staff makes to keep the PHS work culture one of Christian service to others, including one another. Last, the card lists twenty-seven core practices, such as "Avoid thinking and saying, 'It's not my job.' Our job is to serve others, whatever it takes." The practices are reviewed, one every day, followed by a prayer or an inspirational thought at the end of Stand Up.

Says Cathy Bergland, executive director of operations and quality systems and a member of PHS's twelve-person senior management team: "We have no better opportunity to influence how people should think when they are at work, how we want them to treat people, and what kind of culture we want to have here than to have them in Stand Up every day. . . . This truly is a faith-based organization. We are encouraged by and believe strongly in living out our faith at work and meeting the real needs of older adults."

The Leadership Institute helps Presbyterian Homes management and supervisory employees gain skills and competencies needed for effective leadership to reach the organization's goals. Classes are designed to promote and develop the ministry focus of PHS as well as technical competence, high quality of care, and excellence in customer service.

In addition, Presbyterian Homes & Services has increased its commitment over the years to employee training and development, providing regular opportunities to improve knowledge and skills for delivering consistently high-quality services. Standardized training for all 2,700 employees at regional hubs in Minnesota, Wisconsin, and Iowa is coordinated through the PHS Education and Development staff. Employees participate in integrated programs on customer service, communication skills, and special needs of residents. All employees participate in annual training as required by state and federal regulations.

ANSWERING THE CALL

Half a century after its founding, Presbyterian Homes & Services continues to honor its original mission. Though the PHS continuum of care communities are much more sophisticated than that first modest home for thirty of God's servants on the shores of Lake Johanna, the heart of Presbyterian Homes—its purpose and values—remains the same.

"We continue to implement our vision, meeting the needs of older adults of all income levels, from all walks of life and backgrounds, and to provide services in response to our biblical calling and mandate," says Dan Lindh. "As we look to the future, we see continued growth at Presbyterian Homes. Not enormous growth, but enough growth to meet our share of the needs, to be reflective and representative as an organization faithful to this call—to meet our part, if you will, of the burgeoning needs of older adults and to do it in a proactive way, consistent with our purpose, and to do it in a way that can model to other organizations what kinds of things might be possible.

"In meeting those needs, we're going to get involved in other parts of the broader community. We may be involved in educating workers. We're probably going to be involved with employee or workforce housing. We're probably going to be involved in the community in accelerating the use of technology. Right now, we have many 'silos'—different government agencies that have different perspectives, each one trying to meet a niche of the overall changing demand. The challenge in the future is going to be to realign all of the individual organizations and government entities that are involved in older-adult services and to integrate them and focus them on where the needs really are.

"There are a lot of things that change—technology, workforce issues, community needs, kinds of medical services and funding, the face and focus of philanthrophy. We plan to continue to expand, to partner and address the needs and concerns that are increasing in our commuities. What stays the same for us, and what we believe is timeless, is our biblical call to service. We want to serve from the heart. We want to serve because we're called to that service, and we want to make a difference—physically, emotionally, socially, and spiritually. That's what we're called to do, and that's where we'll stay focused in terms of purpose."

APPENDIX 1

PRESBYTERIAN HOMES & SERVICES TIMELINE

1943: Dr. Irving Adams West becomes pastor of the House of Hope Presbyterian Church in St. Paul, Minnesota.

1946: The Synod of Minnesota of the United Presbyterian Church appoints a committee to establish a home for elderly Presbyterians in Minnesota.

1948: Dr. Edwin Kagin becomes president and chair of the Presbyterian Homes board.

1952: Dr. Irving Adams West becomes chair and president of the Presbyterian Homes board.

1952: Presbyterian Homes of the Synod of Minnesota is incorporated.

1955: The Presbyterian Home opens in Arden Hills, Minnesota.

1955: Arthur L. Breidenbach becomes superintendent.

1958: First housing addition opens.

1963: Second housing addition—the Irving Adams West Wing—opens.

1964: Newton Park is added.

1965: Reverend Harry Dodgson becomes superintendent.

1966: Putnam Memorial Chapel opens.

1969: Executive Committee becomes policy-making body only, with four administrative committees. The Presbyterian Home admission fee is eliminated.

1970: The Volunteer Steering Committee is formed.

1970: Reverend K. William Hagstrom becomes superintendent.

1972: Newton Wing and McKnight Dining Room open.

1972: Organization's name changes to Presbyterian Homes of the State of Minnesota.

1978: McKnight Care Center opens in Arden Hills, Minnesota.

1980: Sutton Place opens in Arden Hills, Minnesota.

1984: Dr. B. J. Kennedy becomes chair of the Presbyterian Homes board.

1984: Organization's name changes to the Presbyterian Homes of Minnesota.

1984: Reverend K. William Hagstrom becomes president and CEO. Dr. Irving Adams West becomes honorary chair of the board.

1985: Langton Lake Place (renamed Presbyterian Homes of Roseville in 1992) opens in Roseville, Minnesota.

1985: Gideon Pond Center opens in Bloomington, Minnesota.

1986: Alzheimer's Care Center opens at Langton Lake Place.

1986: Daniel Bolhouse becomes president and CEO of Presbyterian Homes.

1989: Donald E. Garretson becomes chair of the Presbyterian Homes board.

1991: Hugh K. Schilling becomes chair of the Presbyterian Homes board.

1991: Presbyterian Homes acquires Twin Birch Health Care Center and Lakeshore Village in Spring Park, Minnesota, and renames it Presbyterian Homes on Lake Minnetonka.

1991: Rich Road Senior Housing Project (renamed Gideon Pond West and then Ridgeview Terrace) opens in Bloomington, Minnesota.

1991: First Strategic Long Range Plan is adopted.

1992: Names of Presbyterian Homes sites are standardized. Presbyterian Home/Johanna Shores becomes Presbyterian Homes of Arden Hills,

Langton Place becomes Presbyterian Homes of Roseville, Gideon Pond Center becomes Presbyterian Homes of Bloomington, and the Spring Park properties become Presbyterian Homes on Lake Minnetonka.

1993: The Mayfield opens in Little Canada, Minnesota.

1993: Robert H. Bratnober becomes chair of the Presbyterian Homes board.

1994: EagleCrest opens in Roseville, Minnesota, managed by Presbyterian Homes.

1995: Peter Heegard becomes chair of the Presbyterian Homes board.

1995: Beacon Hill opens in Minnetonka, Minnesota.

1995: Presbyterian Homes contracts to manage Echo Ridge in Oakdale, Minnesota.

1995: Presbyterian Homes contracts to manage Central Towers in St. Paul, Minnesota.

1996: Presbyterian Homes contracts to manage Mississippi Shores in Monticello, Minnesota.

1996: Presbyterian Homes contracts to manage Oak Crest in Spring Lake Park, Minnesota.

1997: Donald M. Davies becomes chair of the Presbyterian Homes board.

1997: Daniel A. Lindh becomes president and CEO of Presbyterian Homes.

1997: Presbyterian Homes acquires Eagle Nursing Home in Bloomington, Minnesota, and renames it Bloomington Care Center.

1997: Presbyterian Homes forms Senior Housing Partners, its development arm.

1997: Presbyterian Homes establishes Valley Senior Services Alliance in partnership with Lakeview Hospital and Croixdale.

1998: Presbyterian Homes acquires EagleCrest.

1998: The Farmstead at Andover opens in Andover, Minnesota.

1998: Presbyterian Homes becomes a general partner of Central Towers.

1998: Presbyterian Homes contracts to manage Mill Pond in Ankeny, Iowa.

1999: Organization's name changes to Presbyterian Homes & Services.

1999: PHS acquires Mill Pond.

1999: Avalon Square opens in Waukesha, Wisconsin, under PHS management.

1999: The Deerfield opens in New Richmond, Wisconsin.

1999: PHS acquires Echo Ridge.

1999: Oxboro Project (renamed SummerHouse of Bloomington) opens in Bloomington, Minnesota.

1999: PHS forms Presbyterian Homes Partners with Presbyterian Homes of Wisconsin.

1999: Befriender Nursing Assistant Registered recruitment program is established.

2000: SummerHouse of Woodbury opens in Woodbury, Minnesota.

2000: SummerHouse of Shoreview opens in Shoreview, Minnesota.

2000: PHS contracts to manage Cardinal Pointe in Maplewood, Minnesota.

2001: The Arbor at EagleCrest opens in Roseville, Minnesota.

2001: Kirkland Crossings opens in Pewaukee, Wisconsin, managed by PHS.

2001: St. Andrew's Village opens in Mahtomedi, Minnesota, in partnership with St. Andrew's Evangelical Lutheran Church.

2001: Boutwells Landing opens in Oak Park Heights, Minnesota, in partnership with Lakeview Hospital and Croixdale.

2002: Martin V. Chorzempa becomes chair of the PHS board.

2002: PHS acquires Mississippi Shores.

2002: PHS acquires Castle Ridge.

2002: Presbyterian Homes of Inver Grove Heights opens in Inver Grove Heights, Minnesota.

2002: DOVE training program (Dementia Orientation, Values, and Education) is established.

2002: Empira training program is established.

2003: PHS acquires Oak Crest.

2003: International Nurse Recruitment is implemented.

2003: PHS contracts to manage Avalon Square, which opens in Waukesha, Wisconsin.

2003: The management practice of Stand Up is established.

2004: Highland Ridge opens in Williamsburg, Iowa.

2004: SummerWood of Chanhassen opens in Chanhassen, Minnesota, a PHS partnership with St. Hubert Catholic Church and Catholic Eldercare.

2004: PHS affiliates with Croixdale in Bayport, Minnesota.

2004: PHS acquires The Broadmoor in Eden Prairie.

2004: Sally E. Howard becomes chair of the PHS board.

2004: Presbyterian Homes acquires The Regent in Plymouth, Minnesota, and renames it SummerWood of Plymouth.

2005: The care center at Presbyterian Homes of Bloomington, Minnesota, opens.

2005: Presbyterian Homes of North Oaks, Minnesota, opens.

FUTURE DEVELOPMENTS
(estimated opening dates)

2007: SummerWood of Cottage Grove, Minnesota.

2007: SummerHouse of Roseville, Minnesota.

APPENDIX 2

PRESBYTERIAN HOMES & SERVICES COMMUNITY DIRECTORY

LOCATIONS BY NAME

Avalon Square — IL, AL, MC, HS
Waukesha, Wisconsin

Beacon Hill — IL, AL, HS
Minnetonka, Minnesota

Boutwells Landing — IL, AL, MC , HS
Oak Park Heights, Minnesota

The Broadmoor — IL
Eden Prairie, Minnesota

Cardinal Pointe — IL
Maplewood, Minnesota

Castle Ridge — AL, CC
Eden Prairie, Minnesota

Central Towers — IL, AL, HS
St. Paul, Minnesota

Croixdale — IL, AL, MC, HS
Bayport, Minnesota

The Deerfield — IL, AL, MC, HS
New Richmond, Wisconsin

EagleCrest — IL, AL, MC, HS
Roseville, Minnesota

Echo Ridge — IL
Oakdale, Minnesota

The Farmstead at Andover — IL, AL, MC, HS
Andover, Minnesota

Highland Ridge — IL. AL, MC, HS
Williamsburg, Iowa

Kirkland Crossings — IL, AL, MC, HS
Pewaukee, Wisconsin

The Mayfield — IL
Little Canada, Minnesota

Mill Pond — IL, AL, CC, HS
Ankeny, Iowa

Mississippi Shores — IL
Monticello, Minnesota

Oak Crest — IL
Spring Lake Park

Presbyterian Homes of Arden Hills — IL, AL, MC, CC, HS
Arden Hills, Minnesota

Presbyterian Homes of Bloomington — IL, AL, CC, MC, T/STC, HS
Bloomington, Minnesota

Presbyterian Homes of Inver Grove Heights — IL, AL, MC, HS
Inver Grove Heights, Minnesota

Presbyterian Homes of North Oaks — IL, AL, MC, CC, HS
North Oaks, Minnesota

Presbyterian Homes of Roseville — CC, T/STC, RC, HS
Roseville, Minnesota

Presbyterian Homes on Lake Minnetonka — IL, AL, MC, CC, T/STC, RC, HS
Spring Park, Minnesota

Ridgeview Terrace — IL
Bloomington, Minnesota

St. Andrew's Village — IL, AL, MC, HS
Mahtomedi, Minnesota

SummerHouse of Bloomington — IL, HS
Bloomington, Minnesota

SummerHouse of Shoreview — IL
Shoreview, Minnesota

SummerHouse of Woodbury — IL
Woodbury, Minnesota

SummerWood of of Chanhassen — IL, AL, MC, HS
Chanhassen, Minnesota

SummerWood of Plymouth — IL, AL, MC, HS
Plymouth, Minnesota

KEY

AL – Assisted Living. Apartments, rooms, or suites with housekeeping, personal care, activities, meals.
CC – Care Center. Twenty-four-hour skilled care and support services in semiprivate or private rooms and suites.
HS – Home Services. Skilled care, personal care, rehabilitation therapies, meal preparation, transportation, shopping, housekeeping, and companionship provided to residents in the community.
IL – Independent Living. Townhome or apartment living for older adults seeking a high level of independence with the benefit of a community setting.
MC – Memory Care. In either an assisted living or care center setting, specialized staff and programming for those living with Alzheimer's or dementia.
RC – Respite Care. Temporary care after a hospital stay or rehabilitation program. Also for older adults living with a caregiver needing to be gone temporarily.
T/STC – Transitional/Short Term Care. Intensive skilled care and/or rehabilitation within a care center, including primary skilled care and physical, occupational, speech, and recreational therapies.

LOCATIONS BY CITY AND STATE

IOWA

Ankeny – Mill Pond
Williamsburg – Highland Ridge

MINNESOTA

West Metro

Chanhassen – SummerWood of Chanhassen
Eden Prairie – The Broadmoor, Castle Ridge
Minnetonka – Beacon Hill
Plymouth – SummerWood of Plymouth
Spring Park – Presbyterian Homes on Lake Minnetonka

North Metro

Andover – The Farmstead at Andover
Arden Hills – Presbyterian Homes of Arden Hills
Little Canada – The Mayfield
Monticello – Mississippi Shores
North Oaks – Presbyterian Homes of North Oaks
Roseville – EagleCrest, Presbyterian Homes of Roseville
Shoreview – SummerHouse of Shoreview
Spring Lake Park – Oak Crest

East Metro

Bayport – Croixdale
Mahtomedi – St. Andrew's Village
Maplewood – Cardinal Pointe (managed only)

East Metro (continued)

Oakdale – Echo Ridge
Oak Park Heights – Boutwells Landing
St. Paul – Central Towers
Woodbury – SummerHouse of Woodbury

South Metro

Bloomington – Presbyterian Homes of Bloomington, Ridgeview Terrace, SummerHouse of Bloomington
Inver Grove Heights – Presbyterian Homes of Inver Grove Heights

WISCONSIN

New Richmond – The Deerfield
Pewaukee – Kirkland Crossings
Waukesha – Avalon Square

MORE INFORMATION ABOUT
Presbyterian Homes & Services can be found on the Internet at www.preshomes.org.

FOR INFORMATION ABOUT
member organizations and housing and services for older adults, call Presbyterian Association of Homes and Services for the Aging toll-free at 866-620-6100.

PRESBYTERIAN HOMES & SERVICES BOARD AND ADMINISTRATION

2005 Officers

CHAIR	Ms. Sally E. Howard
IMMEDIATE PAST CHAIR	Mr. Martin V. Chorzempa
VICE CHAIR	Mr. Michael C. Bingham
SECRETARY	Ms. Janna R. Severance
TREASURER	Mr. Robert S. Dunbar

2005 Directors

Mr. Michael C. Bingham
Mr. Larry A. Carlson
Mr. Austin Chapman
Mr. Theodore Chien
Mrs. Megan A. Doyle
Mr. Robert S. Dunbar
Ms. Sandra S. Hawley
Ms. Sally E. Howard
Rev. Linda C. Loving
Mrs. Carole Mae Olson
Mr. John G. Serier
Ms. Janna R. Severance
Mrs. Cara N. Torseth
Mr. Scott A. Weicht
Rev. Dr. Philip C. Brown, Synod Representative (Ex-Officio)

Administrators

Superintendent Arthur L. Breidenbach	1955–1965
Superintendent Rev. Harry Dodgson	1965–1970
Superintendent Rev. K. William Hagstrom (becomes president & CEO in 1984)	1970–1986
President & CEO Daniel Bolhouse	1986–1996
President & CEO Daniel A. Lindh	1997–

Arthur L. Breidenbach.

Rev. Harry Dodgson.

Rev. K. William Hagstrom.

Daniel Bolhouse.

Daniel A. Lindh.

Board Chairs 1955–2005

Dr. Edwin Kagin	1948–1952
Dr. Irving A. West	1952–1984
Dr. B. J. Kennedy	1984–1989
Mr. Donald E. Garretson	1989–1991
Mr. Hugh K. Schilling	1991–1993
Mr. Robert H. Bratnober	1993–1995
Mr. Peter Heegaard	1995–1997
Mr. Donald M. Davies	1997–2001
Mr. Martin V. Chorzempa	2002–2003
Ms. Sally Howard	2004–

Dr. Edwin Kagin.

Dr. Irving A. West.

Dr. B. J. Kennedy.

Donald E. Garretson.

Hugh K. Schilling.

Robert H. Bratnober.

Peter Heegaard.

Donald M. Davies.

Martin V. Chorzempa.

Sally E. Howard.

This book was designed by

Mary Susan Oleson
NASHVILLE, TENNESSEE